THE PASSIONATE

Notes, recipes and anecdotes from the
International Bread Company

By
Paul Homeniuk, Founder & Baker

Bread & friends are a great pair.

Paul Homeniuk

Published by Paul Homeniuk
222 Ridge Rd
East Lansing, MI 48823
Email plr567@msn.com

ISBN # 978-0-9791625-0-3

Introduction

The baking of bread is not for the faint of heart. This is not to say that it is difficult or somehow daunting. I simply point out that it is an activity that requires, even demands, passion. The baking of bread should be done with a sense of purpose, challenge and joy. When possible it should be approached in mass, with family, friends or loved ones involved. When done alone it should be against a background of Wagnerian opera or Bob Seeger like Rock & Roll with your own voice giving sound to the passion of your hands as you work the living tissue that will form your bread.

It is a passion that should be shared both in it's creation and in it's consuming. The baking of fine bread requires time but it is not time consuming. (Time consuming implies that you are somehow wasting time)

Nothing is wasted in the baking of bread, especially time. The history of mankind coming together in communities is the very history of sharing the creating and the consuming of bread.

Within these pages it is my intent to show you the path to great bread making and along the way the forging of bonds that go far beyond the mundane act of putting something in the oven to just nourish the body.

If you are ready to be passionate and to joyously share that passion with others then come along and plunge your hands and your spirit into the world of bread!

Paul Homeniuk

CONTENTS

Section 1 - In the beginning there was great hunger or *"Which of you wants to try chewing on this funny looking grass first"* - Grains and flours unveiled.

Section 2 - Bubble , bubble , toil & trouble or *"Honey, I told you not to leave your gruel sitting out in the sun"* - Leavening & sourdoughs, there is a difference.

Section 3 - Humph? How did you get it to look like that or *"Junior, I told you not to play with that, it is going to be our supper"* - Shapes and how they can change both texture and taste.

Section 4 - The measure of a baker or *"Did you really say you are going to make bread out of six eggs and some flowers?"* - The Formulas. (alright, the bread recipes)

Section 5 - Humankind's struggle to reach beyond the known or *"Damn, this is good but what can we have with it?"* - Soups and creating a meal around bread.

Section 6 - Enhancing taste not covering it up or *"What do you think will happen if we mix this and that?"*
- Spreads, butters, and sundries.

Section 7 - Man does not live by bread alone or *"I didn't know you could do that with chocolate!?"* – A few desserts and other sweet treats.

Section 8 - Miscellaneous thoughts, trivia and resources or *"I bake therefore I am"* - Good things to know.

Index to Recipes

SECTION ONE

In the beginning there was great hunger or *"Which of you wants to try chewing on this funny looking grass first"* - Grains and flours unveiled.

When you think about it, some of the bravest acts of our ancestors must have been trying to eat "foods" that were previously unknown to them. Imagine the first of our progenitors to pluck a snail off a tree and say, "Hey! I wonder what this tastes like?". It was either courage or desperation. My father always told me that if I was hungry enough I would eat anything. We can assume that watching the herd animals graze probably provided some measure of security and mitigated the risk but I like to think it was courage none the less.

It has been long believed that Hunter/Gatherers spent most of their existence looking for food. New theories and evidence seem to put that idea to rest. A family group could and did gather enough acorns to feed themselves for a month in just a few days. Acorn flour is in fact one of the most balanced nutrition substances known to man. Grains wild and later domesticated added another relatively easy nutrition element but not a lot of flavor variety until grinding and milling were applied. Once you had flour there were a wealth of things you could do with it and that would have spurred more creativity.

I want to spend a few moments talking about the different types of flour available today. It is worth noting that Stone ground flours are to be preferred as the milling process generates less heat and therefore does not reduce the nutritional value as much as the hotter steel ground processes more commonly used today. Whole grains include more of the natural plant elements, the husk, the kernel/endosperm.

The French and indeed most of Europe have a distinct advantage in buying flour. They use a classification system where the buyer can know that if he/she is buying Number 65 flour it will have a specific ash content and other specs regardless of which brand or mill they are buying from. The United States has never adopted that sort of standardization and so it is difficult for the discerning baker to know which American Brands have what specifications.

In general, the lower protein levels are used for cakes, pastry etc. As you move up in protein you hit All-Purpose flours then Bread Flours then whole grains. The cake and all-purpose flours also have a lower ash content. Ash levels are determined by burning a specified amount of flour at really, really high temperatures and then scraping up and measuring the amount of residue. The bulk of the minerals (ash) is contained in the germ and the husk (bran) of the grain therefore it makes sense that higher protein flours have higher ash contents.

Flour also contains enzymes that determine the rates that starches are turned into sugar therefore making them available for those hungry little yeast to use. More about yeast in Section two!

A few flour basics (there are a lot more but these will let you start baking good bread):

Whole wheat flour - A simple description and type. It is flour made from milling the entire kernel of wheat. The husk, the germ every part of the wheat head goes in and is left in after the milling. Nothing is sifted out.

All-Purpose flour is a low protein white flour where usually the bran or husk is not milled or is sifted out after milling. In the United States it also usually means that the flour has been bleached of most nutrients and had them re-introduced artificially (apparently just because they can!?)

Bread Flour is a higher protein and ash level. Often white but can be whole grain. Many U.S. brands market it labeled as "bread flour".

Patent flour or Clear flour. There was a time were these two were different but in the U.S. at least they have come to mean the same thing. Both are extremely high protein flours milled exclusively from the central part of the endosperm that have in many cases had additional gluten introduced.

Rye flour is milled from rye grass. Rye has an extremely low gluten level and so must be blended with a high protein wheat flour such as Clear to be used for successful bread making. If you tried to make a 100 percent pure rye bread you would end up with a brick that does not rise. Another foible of rye is that it contains a very starchy, viscous substance that can interfere with the formation of the gluten and becomes very glue like and sticky when introduced to water. This is why really good rye bread uses a sour starter that is wheat based. The fermentation can get well on it's way before the yeast come in contact with the sticky, gluey stuff (I admit it. I don't know the scientific name for this glue like substance).

Oat Flour is becoming more widely available because of the many health properties of oats. It can make some wonderful breads but will also need to be combined with some wheat flour. Oat flour is flaky in texture if not temperament.

These are the basics that will let you get started. Graham flour is essentially whole wheat flour that has been milled a little finer. Find a good All-Purpose flour and a good Bread flour and you can be well prepared for most home bread baking. A little bakers tip for checking the relative protein levels (remember, higher protein = higher gluten) is to take a handful of flour and squeeze it very tightly in your fist. When you open your hand if the flour stays in a big clump it is lower in protein. If the flour crumbles back into a handful of loose flour it is higher in protein.

SECTION TWO

Bubble, bubble, toil & trouble *or "Honey, I told you not to leave your gruel sitting in the sun." –*
Leavening & sourdoughs, there is a difference.

Okay, the answer to the big question is.......

Everyone asks, what is the difference between yeast and sour dough? The answer is **civilization and breeding.** Sour dough is yeast and yeast is sour dough. Before I explain the difference let me tell you about those wonderful little beasties called yeast.

Yeast is probably the most prevalent life form on the planet. Every time you take a breath you suck in hundreds of thousands of the little critters. They are every where. Many varieties exist but only a handful or two are good for bread. Fortunately they are the most common varieties out there. *(Trivia note - San Francisco sour dough is made with a distinct strain of yeast that is found only in a very small area around San Francisco. Some estimate that it's habitat is less than two square miles. So, unless your "true" San Francisco sour dough was baked in San Francisco or the yeast imported from San Francisco, the baker used flavorings and additives to fake the real thing.)*

Yeast are very single minded creatures. They live and die just to eat, excrete and reproduce. It is this living variable that makes baking bread so exciting to me. Because you are dealing with a living organism of multiple varieties you never know exactly how things will turn out from one loaf to the next. Yeast is hearty. They can be dried and stored, even frozen after they have been dried and kept for centuries, then reconstituted with a little water and nourishment and used to bake wonderful bread. When most people think of yeast they are thinking of the dry or fresh variety you purchase in a store. These factory farmed yeasts have the advantage of being controlled as to what variety they are and can be concentrated through growth and in the case of fresh yeast storage in an agar medium. They allow very consistent results.

Sour dough is essentially wild yeast. If you mix a little flour and water together to make a paste and leave it sit for twenty four to forty eight hours, it will become home for many of the yeast floating around out there. It will begin to ferment and bubble and produce carbon dioxide (which is what makes a bread rise) and alcohol and water and proteins and acids and all sorts of wondrous little natural chemical stews.

In European tradition it is common for a baker when starting a new sour dough to take a wooden spoon and wooden bowl add some flour and water and maybe a slice of pear and then take an early morning stroll through the meadows, fields or woodlands around their shop. They will stir the mixture and enjoy the day as they collect the native, wild yeasts in their bowl to begin their lives as un-paid employees of the baker. From a scientific perspective you can probably pick up the same yeasts in your own kitchen by opening the window but most bakers that I know and respect swear they get a better sour by taking their stroll.

Sour dough need to be fed regularly. If you bake often, just add a little fresh flour and water to your sour on a regular basis and keep it in a warm safe place and most will do fine. If you don't bake that often but are really pleased with the sour you have created you can paint some on a piece of plastic wrap in a thin coating. Allow it to dry and then put it in the freezer or mail it to a friend to try. When ready to use again just scrape the dry sour off the plastic wrap, add a little water and a touch of sugar to get things going and within a day or so your yeast will come out of the dormant state and begin doing what they do best!

Please note that you can freeze dry yeast but **do not freeze fresh yeast**. Fresh yeast is full of moisture and moisture expands when frozen and so the tiny little cell walls of your yeast will pop like a cheap balloon killing it rather than putting it into hibernation.

Let me talk about sours, leavens, bigas, poolish etc. These are essentially names in different languages for the same thing. They are sour dough starters. Some may be dough like some may be soupy. They are all fermentation methods to make bread rise. It is important to note that yeast do more than just produce carbon dioxide to cause bread to rise. The fermentation process creates a variety of acids, proteins and enzymes that affect flavor and texture and longevity of the finished loaf. The longer a dough rises the longer the finished bread will stay fresh. The natural acids and proteins produced by the fermentation serve as preservatives. Shops that use proofing cabinets manage to hurry the rise but they do not get the acids and proteins and so they have to add preservatives which are usually fat or oil based.

Poolish is worth some special mention. It was a method created to speed up the fermentation process and make it a little more easy to care for and feed. It basically calls for flour and water to be mixed with a small amount of yeast (wild or otherwise) and allowed to ferment overnight before use. This creates a very active leavening that can be made in quantity as soon as the night before baking. This technique was created by Polish bakers and was actually known simply as "The Polish method". At the time though, the rest of the world had a number of bias against the Polish people and did not like to give them credit for what had quickly become one of the great improvements in modern baking. The name was corrupted to the "poolish method" and later just "poolish" so that the originators did not have to acknowledged.

Many of the bread recipes in this book will use poolish or some other sour starter. Some will be specific to the bread but nearly all can be interchanged. Don't be bashful about trying your own sour creations. The amount you need may vary but you can have a profound change in flavor, texture, crust and crumb by changing the "sour" in a recipe without changing anything else. It's fun, try it. You'll like it!

So lets recap - Sour and yeast are both yeast. One is farmed and one is wild. The longer you ferment the better the bread and the longer the bread will stay fresh. Sours can be dough like stiff or pasty or thin and soupy. In this book, when we say yeast we mean fresh, factory produced yeast not dried

SECTION THREE

How did you get it to look like that or "Junior, I told you not to play with that, it is going to be our supper" - Shapes and how they can change both texture and taste.

Shaping of dough plays a greater role than just making a uniform loaf. The shape of a loaf can have an effect on the texture and flavor of a bread. The Italians even have a name for an entire class of breads based on the unusual shapes The most basic shapes needed for the baking of good bread are called "Loose Ball" and "Tight Ball". Nearly every loaf will start as either a loose or tight ball to relax the dough before final shaping. "Boule" is French for "ball" or "round" and it is the most basic shape used in French breads. A French baker of breads is called a *"Boulanger"* A maker of rounds.

The classic baguette shape *(the baguette was invented in Vienna but the French adopted it with a passion)* is the next most common shape in French bread. Between a Boule and a Baguette there is a *"Batard"* or bastard. It is neither Boule nor baguette but something in between hence it's name.

A loose ball is the shape most often used after the dough has had it's initial rise. The dough is simply stretched around and under to make a smooth ball with a taut, tear free surface. The key thing here is to use the palm or flat of your hand rather than your fingers which may cause rips and tears in the surface of the dough. If shaping on a workbench or table you may use the sides of your hands to catch a little "lip" of dough and stretch underneath to the bottom center of the piece of dough.

A tight ball is used where a tighter more even crumb is desired. The dough is taken and scaled and then slightly flattened into a rough rectangle. It is then rolled jelly roll style then the log is shaped into a round as you would a loose ball.

It is important to note that dough can be very forgiving but it should be pressed into shape rather than pounded into shape. Pressing the dough allows the bubbles of gas that have caused it to rise to shift and move. Pounding the dough will pop the bubbles and deflate the dough.

A **dough knife** is essential to the shaping of fine breads. It should be an extension of your arm when working with the dough. Picking up a piece of dough that has been rising on a counter with your fingers quite often results in rips, tears and stretching and gouges. All these things deflate the dough and each tear in the surface creates a weakness that will cause the loaf to burst in unexpected and unwanted ways when baked. Scooping a piece of dough with a dough knife solves all of these potential problems.

Even a bread that is going into a loaf pan for baking is allowed to rest and rise in a ball. The shaping of the ball helps to give the dough a smooth, even surface which will in turn become a pleasing crust. Many shapes are specific to individual breads. Lets look at a few starting with the baguette.

This classic long thin loaf was created when bakers had just learned how to create a thin, crisp crust by using injectable steam in their ovens. This famous crust that falls into tiny razor shards when broken became all the rage. People wanted more of this wonderful crust and so the baguette was created to increase the ratio of crust to crumb. (Crumb being what the inside of a loaf is called) A versatile bread it has become the hallmark of a baker's skill. In competition the finished, cooled loaf must be 250 grams plus or minus 5 grams. A baker must know his dough and understand how much weight will be lost in baking. The shape will have a profound effect on the weight loss as a longer loaf has more surface area for the moisture (weight) to be lost.

Learning to shape a baguette is like learning to play chess. Someone can show you the basic moves in just a few moments but it can take a life time to master them.

Some other classic shapes for basic loaves include the Pouches (La tabatiere), Tricorns, Caps, Braids, Spirals, Crowns and Crowns Lyonnaises, Bear Claws (Les pattes d'ours), Horseshoes and Crescents. You can use a single dough to make each of these shapes and the finished bread will have different texture in crumb and crust and in many cases different flavor. This is because the surface area has changed and so drying and evaporating in the baking is altered. The crust will be thinner or thicker based on the shape, this in turn will effect the flavor as thinner areas will become more caramelized and crisper. Don't forget that yeast is a living organism and that shapes will have an effect on how easily they spread and reproduce in a loaf and this to will also effect the flavor and texture.

The shaping of bread can also be done strictly for decorative purposes. Entire competitions are built on creating edible sculptures, I have seen everything from Zen temples beneath a blossoming cherry tree to cuckoo clocks. The book, "Special and Decorative Breads" by Roland Bilheux, Alan Escoffier, Daniel Herve' and Jean-Marie Pouradier is an excellent tool for anyone wishing to learn about this art.

To review some key points. Shaping does make a difference. Smooth balls, loose or tight, with a smooth unbroken surface will give you the nicest looking finished loaf. Different shapes can make a difference in both taste and texture. Like most other things in life, the more you do it the better you get.

A final note on shaping. We should mention "slashing". This is done for both decorative purpose and to control the break as the bread bakes and expands in the oven. A very sharp knife will work but a lame with a razor blade is best. The lame is a small handle with a curve in the blade holder (The King Arthur Flour catalog offers a nice but expensive one). This makes it easier to undercut as you make your slashes in your dough. Specific types of slashes are discussed in the individual bread recipes. A slash should always be one smooth, single stroke. Do not jab or hack!

When a loaf has been shaped, it should, unless otherwise noted rest and be baked with the seam side down. Ideally, your seam should always be centered and down.

SECTION FOUR

The measure of a baker or "Did you really say you are going to make bread out of 6 eggs and some flowers?" - The Formulas (alright, recipes)

First let us set a few conventions, ground rules and definitions. Each of the formulas being offered up here are set in batches of 2 if they are bread and 12 if they are rolls. You should never make less than two loaves of bread at a time as that would be down right uncivilized. If you cannot eat them both give one away. If you are baking with friends or loved ones there should be no problem here. Remember the baking and enjoying of bread achieves it's greatest glory when it is shared.

We weigh all ingredients as opposed to measuring volume. The moisture content of flour can vary immensely and humidity and your mood can all effect the dough. By weighing ingredients you can keep the hydration level (amount of water vs. dry ingredients) consistent and it is easier to scale to different batch sizes! A nice balance scale is great but a $15.99 plunger style diet/kitchen scale will work just fine for most home bakers.

We have tried to list the liquid ingredients last in each formula as the actual liquid may vary with the humidity of the room, the flour, the grain itself and the mood of the baker. These variations are why liquid is always added last so you can make adjustments if needed to get the consistency of the dough that you want. Always hold back a little of the liquid until you see how the dough is coming together. You can always add more but it is really, really hard to take some out!

We take for granted that all temperatures are based on you pre-heating your oven and having it fully up to temperature before putting any loaf in.

Stone is an incredible surface to bake on. If you are baking commercially use a stone decked oven for bread. If you are baking at home get a stone for your oven. A pizza stone will work but see if you can get your local stone mason to cut you a piece of European limestone to fit your oven shelf squarely. European is needed because the tensile strength is different than North American limestone. The constant heating and cooling will crack and crumble the North American stone many times faster than it will the European. AWMCO INC. In Chicago makes a wonderful synthetic stone for both commercial and home applications. Their phone number is 773 846 1760. They can be found on the web also with full details, pricing and ordering capabilities on-line.

Biga, sponge, Poolish, and many other names are essentially the same thing depending on what country the bread originated in. They are pre-ferments made in what was originally recognized as the Polish method. The word Poolish was essentially a distortion of the phrase "The Polish Method" because there were many at the time who hated to give the Polish credit for a method that has proven so valuable and effective in the baking of bread We use the name used in whatever country the bread recipe originated.

It is a little harder to find but fresh or "cake" yeast is much preferred over dry or granulated yeast. If dry is all you have that is fine but always start it fermenting in a little warm water first. (Really, save yourself the step and buy fresh).

We talk about types of flour in Section One but stock an all-purpose and a higher protein bread flour in your cupboard at all times and you will usually be prepared for what ever baking mood strikes you and yours.

Steam is important for many crusts. There are ways to add a little steam in your home oven but you should know you will never get a near perfect baguette without injectable steam. You can come sort of close in your home oven but you will not quite get there. Please understand that close is still real fine eating so don't hesitate to proceed. If you are baking at home and do not have injectable steam the next best thing you can do is to place an oven safe bowl heaped full of ice on the bottom of your oven just before putting the bread in place.

There is a tendency to open doors to look at how bread is doing. Slap your hand and put a dollar in a jar for every time you open the oven door. Opening the door is going to let hot air out and cold air in. This will do all sorts of strange and interesting things to your bread, especially your crust. The rule is OPEN THE OVEN DOOR AS FEW TIMES AS POSSIBLE!!!

How to tell if a loaf is done. Bake times listed in recipes are a great guess but that is all they are. Ovens, especially home ovens vary so much in temperature and ability to heat evenly that times can only be a guess. The type and size and shape of the loaves you made will have an effect on heating time. <u>The only certain way to tell if a loaf is properly done is to "knock" it.</u>

This technique does not mean that you tell your loaf it is crumby or a crusty old fool. It simply means that you pick the loaf up (use an oven mitt unless you have baker's hands) and knock on the **bottom** of the loaf. If you get a dull thud, put it back and let it finish baking. If you get a nice hollow sound like a drum the loaf is ready to come out from the oven. You should also note that in most crusty, country style loaves when the bread is taken from the oven and put on a rack to cool you will probably hear a soft crackling sound as the cool air of the room caresses the hot crust. This is a good sign that you have a well baked loaf so rejoice!

Key points to recap - Always add liquid last and hold a little back until you see how the dough is starting to come together. You can always add more liquid but your family and friends will think you have lost your mind if you try to take out liquid that has already been added to your flour.

Weighing ingredients keeps hydration levels consistent and makes scaling batch sizes easy. Ovens are always pre-heated and a good baking stone will do wonders for your ego as it will make it easy to produce loaf after loaf of classic breads.

ALE BREAD

This recipe came to us from Belgium and a good Belgian ale is nice to use but any good quality ale will work just fine. I like using the pearl barley to toast but rolled barley will work. The pearl gives a crunchier, nutty texture and flavor while the rolled barley provides a softer texture.

2 Batch
Preheat to 425 degrees
Use dough hook

5/8	Ounce	flour, whole wheat
1 3/4	Ounce	flour, clear
1 3/4	Ounce	water
1/8	Ounce	yeast
1/4	Ounce	yeast
2	Ounce	flour, whole wheat
1 1/4	Pound	flour, bread
3/8	Ounce	salt
1/4	Ounce	malt
1 1/4	Ounce	roasted barley
3/4	Pound	Ale

Spread barley on a tray and roast in 400 degree oven until golden brown. About 20 min. Allow to cool.

BIGA (1st four ingredients)
Dissolve the yeast in water. Mix with other Biga ingredients and place in covered container overnight. This should rise, double and collapse before using.
DOUGH
Place the ale (room temperature) and the biga in mixing bowl. Dissolve the yeast into this mixture. Add the remaining ingredients except the barley to the dough and mix on 1st speed with dough hook until coming clean from the bowl. Add the roasted barley and mix on 2nd speed until smooth. Cover and allow to double.

Divide into two roughly equal pieces, round and allow to rest for twenty minutes.

SHAPING 2 : The Canoe. Place piece bottom side up on work bench. Place small rolling pin or 3/4 inch dowel in center of dough and press down. Roll it slightly from side to side. Pinch the ends of the dough piece together to close the indentation made by the pin. Turn upside down and gently shape by cupping your hands on the bottom of the dough and evenly shaping the piece. Place the dough seam side down on cloth or floured tray and allow to rise about 40 minutes. Turn dough seam side up when peeling or placing into the oven.

BAKE OFF: Fill the oven with steam just before putting the bread in. It is done when it knocks and has a deep golden to dark brown color.

BABKA

This is a Polish recipe that came to us through one of our customer's Grandmother. The name is actually derived from the Polish word for Grandmother. It is very light and as is common in the European tradition not as sweet as you might think. Rich is a more accurate description for this treat that is traditionally served at Easter but is great any time. Yes, it is European so the crust is going to be darker than many Americans are used to but it is wonderful.

2 Batch

SPONGE

½	Ounce	yeast
3/4	Ounce	flour, all-purpose
2/3	Teaspoon	sugar
1 1/4	Ounce	water
3 3/4	Ounce	milk

Preheat to 375 degrees
Use dough hook

DOUGH

4	Each	egg yolk
1	Each	egg
1/3	Teaspoon	salt
1 1/3	Ounce	sugar
1 1/4	Ounce	butter, unsalted -- melted
2/3	Teaspoon	vanilla
½	Teaspoon	lemon peel
5/8	Pound	flour, all-purpose
2	Ounce	raisins (soaked in a little warm water or rum then drained)

SPONGE: Mix sponge ingredients with paddle or wooden spoon. This will be a wet sponge. Allow to rise at room temperature or overnight in refrigerator.

DOUGH: Put sponge in bowl add all other ingredients and mix just until well blended. Should be a soft but not sticky dough. Add flour if needed .

Divide into two roughly equal pieces, round and place in a lightly sprayed Brioche pans.

FINAL RISING: Until about 1 inch above pan, about 30 to 40 minutes.

Bake in center of the oven until done. After removing from oven immediately glaze with a mixture of 1 part warm milk mixed with 1 part powdered sugar.

BAPS

This sturdy little roll from Scotland probably inspired the English muffin. It can easily be stuffed with things such as egg or ham and makes a neat little packet that laborers would carry with them to the fields and later the factories for their lunch. Try them warm from the oven with a little butter, unsalted and honey. You can pack them plain with a nice piece of Cotswold cheese and a good pickle and have a classic "plowman's lunch"

12 Batch

Preheat to 425 degrees
Use dough hook

1 ¼	Pound	flour, bread
1 ½	Tablespoon	salt
2	Ounce	lard (shortening can be used but I love the lard version best)
5/8	Ounce	yeast
½	Teaspoon	sugar
7	Ounce	milk
7	Ounce	water

MIX OFF: Combine all ingredients until smooth silky dough. The dough should be soft but not be sticky. FIRST RISING: Allow to double, covered about 1 hour

SCALING: 3 ounce pieces

SHAPING: Round and then pat into an oval about 4 ½ inches by 3 inches (use flour on your hands if needed) - Place well apart on lightly sprayed baking sheets or use parchment pan liner.
Lightly brush the Baps with milk then sift a fine layer of flour over them.

SECOND RISING: let rise uncovered until doubled, about 30 minutes. DO NOT OVER PROOF

Sift a second fine layer of flour over the tops then press your thumb into the center of each. This technique will make the surface flattish rather than domed.

BAKE OFF: Bake until lightly browned. Approximately 30 Minutes.

BARLEY BREAD

This is an English peasant loaf that the peasants tried hard to keep secret. Barley was a coarse grain more often fed to livestock than to people. The nobility would often only allow their serfs and such to have barley for their own use as it was cheaper than wheat flour. The thing was the people developed a really tasty, really healthy bread from it and kept how good it was a secret in fear that the local lord would take it away from them or worse yet, tax it. I love this one toasted in the morning with a little butter, unsalted and honey.

Preheat to 425 degrees
Use dough hook

2 Batch

1 1/8	Pound	flour, bread
6 ½	Ounce	flour, whole wheat
6 ½	Ounce	flour, Barley
3/4	Ounce	yeast
1	Ounce	salt
1 1/8	Pound	water
2	Ounce	milk

MIX OFF: Mix all ingredients until smooth firm dough

FIRST RISING: Allow to double

SCALING: 2 pound 2 Ounce

SHAPING: Smooth round to short log and place in loaf pan.

FINAL RISING: Until doubled

BAKE OFF: Until sounds hollow when knocked. (about 45 minutes)

BLACK BREAD

This is the classic from Russia dark or "whole rye" flour is used. Even with the dark rye flour you would not get the famous "black" color if something was not used to darken it. This recipe calls for molasses and cocoa. It is not uncommon to find recipes using coffee (some the grounds, some day old strong coffee) or other more exotic things to give it the rich, black look it is known for. Brushing a little salt water on the surface just before baking will give the loaf a wonderful shiny look.

Preheat to 425 degrees
Use dough hook

2 Batch

1 1/8	Pound	flour, dark rye
½	Pound	flour, whole wheat
5 2/3	Ounce	flour, bread
2/3	Ounce	salt
7/8	Ounce	yeast
1/4	Ounce	ginger
1/4	Ounce	cocoa
3 2/3	Tablespoon	molasses
½	Pound	water

MIX OFF : Mix all ingredients on 1st speed. Add additional water if needed to get a smooth dough. Mix about 9 minutes .

FIRST RISING: Until Doubled

SCALE: 1 pound, 12 Ounce or just divide in two.

SHAPING: Smooth balls. When all scaled go back and roll gently into fat cigar about 12 inches long. Cut 4 sausage slit across the tops and allow to rise on well corn-mealed trays.

It is also common to bake this as a round loaf that is slightly flattened. Use a skewer or food thermometer to poke a cross of holes in the top (five one direction three across). This will help control the bake of the round loaf and give you a really nice round of bread

BAKE OFF: Brush with salt water. Best baked directly on stone with steam in the oven. Bake until done Approx. 40 minutes.

BRIOCHE

This recipe came to us from the mother of a good friend. Momma Parisi was an Italian raised in Northern Morocco while it was French colony. She was near eighty years old when she consented to teach me this recipe for use in my shop. It had been in her family for generations and she was very particular about my being able to do it correctly. I did pass the test and it became a customer favorite.

Brioche dates to around 1300 in France. It was created by a baker in honor of the Queen's birthday. The long rising time gives it the rich flavor. Legend has the shape being modeled after part of the queen's anatomy. It was an honorable thing in that time as she was the "Mother of her Country".

Preheat to 400 degrees
Use dough hook.

2 Batch

1	Pound	flour, bread
2 1/8	Ounce	sugar
1/8	Ounce	salt
1/3	Ounce	yeast
3 1/4	Ounce	butter, unsalted, unsalted
3	Each	eggs
1	Each	egg yolk
3 5/8	Ounce	milk

MIX OFF: Combine all ingredients at first speed in mixer bowl until it comes together. Beat on second speed just until it comes clean from the sides and bottom of the bowl. Approximately 9 minutes.

FIRST RISING: Remove to a covered container and allow to rise overnight in refrigerator. Twenty hours of rising at this point is idea.

Divide into two roughly equal pieces. Pinch off about 1 Ounce (about the size of a walnut). Shape larger piece into loose ball and place in Brioche mold. Roll smaller piece into ball and pinch and roll a small neck onto it. Using thumb make indentation just off center in top of large piece. Insert neck of small piece into indentation and press to seal.

Brush well with egg glaze made of two egg whites and a tablespoon of sugar.
Allow to rise uncovered until doubled.
BAKE-OFF: Bake at 375 degrees for approximately 45 minutes.
NOTE: Traditionally this would get a second coating of the glaze just before going in the oven. This would give a very dark, chocolate brown crust which is considered normal for this bread. You can skip the second glaze and go with a lighter "Americanized" crust with no problem.

CAKE WITH HAM & OLIVE

This is a wonderful variation that crops up throughout France. One couple who came to the store regularly noted that they would slice a loaf of this bread, make a pitcher of Martinis and sit by the pool for the entire day. They noted "life doesn't get any better". We like it as part of a Holiday snack or breakfast when friends and family are staying over. This is very rich!

Preheat to 350 degrees
Use the paddle attachment for your mixer.

2 Batch

5/8	Pound	flour, all-purpose
1	Tablespoon	baking powder
5/8	Cup	white wine -- dry
5/8	Cup	vermouth -- dry
4 ½	Each	egg -- beaten
7 ½	Ounce	olive oil
7 3/4	Ounce	ham -- diced
5 3/4	Ounce	Gruyere cheese
7 3/4	Ounce	green olive -- chopped

Add flour, baking powder, wine, vermouth and eggs. Mix on first speed just until incorporated.

Add olive oil a bit at a time until you have a smooth, thick batter. Add the ham, cheese and olives, mixing just until incorporated.

Scrape the batter into 8 x 4 inch loaf pans. Bake until loaf is golden brown and a toothpick inserted in center emerges clean. (about 55 minutes)

Cool briefly then invert and remove loaf. Allow to cool completely on wooden racks.

CHOCOLATE ZUCCHINI BREAD

Kelly Urbaniak came to work at the shop in the summer of 1999 while she was in college. She proved to be a wonderful employee and friend. Starting as general counter help she later became my apprentice and shared in the baking duties until she graduated. She was sharp, fun, a hard worker and insistent that we try this zucchini bread recipe. I had my doubts but had a great deal of respect for Kelly. The bread proved to be great and soon became a favorite with many of our customers.

2 Batch

Preheat to 375 degrees.
Use the paddle attachment for your mixer.

7/8	Pound	flour, bread
2 7/8	Each	egg
1	Pound	sugar
7 3/4	Ounce	oil
1	Teaspoon	vanilla
1	Teaspoon	cinnamon
1	Teaspoon	baking soda
1	Teaspoon	baking powder
4	Ounce	sour cream
1	Pint	zucchini -- chopped
7 3/4	Ounce	chocolate -- semi-sweet

The secret to this bread is to not chop the zucchini too fine. If you have a mandolin with a large julienne blade this will work great. If using a knife, about a 1/4 inch dice is idea.

Blend the flour, sugar, baking soda and baking powder together first to ensure even distribution. Then add all the other ingredients and mix just until well blended.

Scrape batter into 8 x 4 inch loaf pans that have been very lightly sprayed or oiled.

Bake until a skewer inserted in center comes out clean (except perhaps for some melted chocolate). About 30 to 40 minutes.

CIABATTA

This is the classic Italian "Slipper" bread. Legend has that it resembles the bottom or "shoe" part of the map of Italy hence the name Ciabatta or Slipper. This uses a Lievito Naturale. This is simply another type of Poolish (see section 2). This is more dough like then most Poolish and should be made the day before it is to be used. Let it ferment in the refrigerator where it will have to work harder and produce all the wonderful acids, proteins and enzymes that will make this a truly extraordinary bread.

2 Batch

LIEVITO NATURALE (make 1 day ahead)

1	Pound	Flour, all-purpose
3/8	Ounce	yeast
6	Ounce	water -- warmed

Put all the water in the mixer (should be about body temperature) and the yeast. Start mixer on 1st speed and add the flour a bit at a time. Keep adding the flour until you have a very stiff but smooth dough. Place into a bowl, covered and allow to rise over night in the refrigerator.

Preheat to 400 degrees
Use dough Hook

DOUGH

1 1/8	Pound	Lievito Naturale
7/8	Pound	flour, bread
7/8	Pound	water
½	Ounce	salt
½	Ounce	yeast
½	Ounce	powdered milk

MIXING: Add all the ingredients(including the lievito naturale) to the bowl except about 20 % of the water. Mix for 6 minutes on first speed.

Change speed to second and mix for 10 minutes. During the last 6 minutes add the remaining water. You want a moist, very wet dough. This will not be fun to work with! Strew a lot of flour on the bench, take the dough out of the bowl divide it in two roughly equal pieces.

Shape into flat rectangles about 5 inches by 14 inches. Keep the loaves as rectangular as possible.

Let the loaves rise on the well-floured surface of the bench for 30 minutes.

FLATTENING: Dimple each loaf with the finger tips several times and flip over. You want to have little indentations. This should be a flattish rectangle.

FINAL RISING: Allow to rise 25 minutes. BE PRECISE ON THIS TIME

Gently move the loaves directly on to the oven stone. Bake approx. 25 minutes until golden brown.

COCONUT BREAD

More cake than bread. This loaf is found in various forms throughout the West Indies. This was one of those loafs that when we made it at the shop, no matter how many we made we would sell out and leave the late comers disappointed. I lost count of how many times I heard customers say, "I don't like coconut but I love this bread!" It has a dark golden crust that is crunchy and toasty but a moist cake like interior that will crumble into flavorful sweetness.

2 Batch

Preheat to 375 degrees
Use paddle attachment.

6 3/8	Ounce	coconut
1 1/3	Pound	flour, all-purpose
1 3/4	Tablespoon	baking powder
2 3/8	Teaspoon	vanilla extract
1 1/4	Teaspoon	salt
2/3	Pound	sugar
2/3	Pound	butter, unsalted
2/3	Cup	coconut milk
2/3	Cup	milk

The most common problem people have with baking this bread is that it collapses in the middle as it cools. There are two things that should happen to prevent this. First make certain that your butter, unsalted is at room temperature. Second do not under bake the loaf. The crust will get a light mahogany brown. I always told my staff that this is one of those breads that when you think it is done, give it another ten minutes. It is truly worth the wait.

Blend the butter, unsalted and all dry ingredients together until well coated in the butter, unsalted. Add the milks and the vanilla and beat on medium speed until you have a thick, pasty batter. This will not pour from the bowl. You will need to scoop it into your lightly sprayed or oiled loaf pans. Level the batter as best you can (use your fingers if needed).

Bake in middle of oven until done (see above). Allow to cool for approximately 20 minutes before removing from pan or slicing.

CORN BREAD

This is our popular Mexican corn bread. Some folks prefer to leave the Jalapeno out but I think at least a little is an absolute necessity for integrating all the other flavors. My daughter Rachel insists that more cheese is an acceptable substitute for the pepper. The point is that you shouldn't be afraid to modify this to your own tastes. *Hi Ken! You can leave the onion out with no problem and be 100% "Ken Safe".*

2 Batch

Preheat to 375 degrees
Use the paddle attachment

3/4	Pound	corn meal
3/4	Ounce	flour, all-purpose
1	Ounce	sugar
½	Ounce	salt
1 1/4	Tablespoons	baking powder
4	Ounce	powdered milk
3	Each	eggs
3/4	Pound	water
1	Pound	creamed corn
1/3	Cup	jalapeno -- drained & diced
6	Ounce	cheddar cheese -- grated
1/3	Each	onion -- grated
4	Ounce	oil

Combine all ingredients until well moistened. This will give you a thick batter.

Pour batter into lightly sprayed or oiled loaf pans.

BAKE OFF: 375 degrees. Bake until golden brown and a skewer comes out of center clean (about 50 minutes)

CORNISH SAFFRON CAKE

This is one of life's great pleasures. Warm from the oven or toasted in the morning and drizzled with honey this bread is the basis of the term "comfort food". We adapted it from a 400 year old treatise on English baking.

2 Batch

Preheat to 375 degrees
Use dough hook

1 2/3	Pound	flour, bread
3/4	Ounce	yeast
7	Ounce	butter, unsalted
3 3/8	Ounce	sugar
1 5/8	Teaspoon	salt
3 3/8	Ounce	raisin (personally I like to use golden raisins)
½	Teaspoon	nutmeg
3/8	Teaspoon	cinnamon
½	Pound	milk
7/8	Teaspoon	saffron threads

Heat about 2 ounces of milk just until it starts to foam at the edges. Crumble the saffron into the milk and allow to sit at least 30 minutes.
Allow remaining milk to come to room temperature.

Allow the butter, unsalted to come to room temperature.

Place all other ingredients into mixer bowl. blend in the soften butter, unsalted on low speed. At the milk and saffron mixture. Add remaining milk to get a soft but not runny dough.

Allow to rise until doubled.

Divide the dough into two pieces

Gently shape each piece into a smooth log and place into a lightly sprayed loaf pan. Allow to rise until just mounding above the edge of the pan..

Bake in center of oven until the loaf "knocks". Approximately 30 to 40 minutes
As soon as removed from oven brush the loafs with a mixture of equal parts warm milk and powdered sugar.

Allow to cool 15 minutes in the pan before turning out of pan.

DEVONSHIRE SPLITS

We went looking for a recipe for these little gems at the request of a customer of ours from Devonshire, England. Once we added them to our line-up they became a real hit. One day another customer came to me and said, "These are pretty good but you really should try the Cornish Splits, they are so much better." Curious, I went looking for Cornish Split recipes. I found a bundle of them. All of them differed from the Devonshire splits by a mere fraction of butter, unsalted or sugar. It just goes to show we become very attached to those items we think of as "ours". You don't have to be from Cornwall or Devon to enjoy these versatile little rolls!

12 Batch
Preheat to 400 degrees
Use dough hook

3 7/8	Pound	flour, bread
1 1/8	Ounce	salt
1 ½	Ounce	yeast
1 1/4	Ounce	sugar
5/8	Pound	butter, unsalted
2 1/8	Pound	milk

Mix milk and yeast in bowl. Let stand until frothy.

Add flour, salt, sugar and butter, unsalted mix on first speed until you have a soft but not sticky dough.
Knead about 5 minutes longer to get a smooth and elastic dough.

Cover dough and allow to double, about 1 1/2 hours.

Gently scale the dough into 2 ounce pieces. Use your dough knife.

Lightly spray and then dust baking sheets with flour or use parchment pan liners.

Shape into smooth ball by rolling in your hands or on work table. Arrange rolls on baking tray so that they are almost (but not) touching. 12 to a tray. It is very important to have even rows as they will expand to touch each other and even rows assure equal size rolls.

Cover rolls with slightly damp towel and let rise 45 minutes.

400 degrees. Bake the splits for 20 to 30 minutes or until golden brown.

Remove the rolls from oven and immediately sift confectioners sugar over the rolls. Cover with dry towel and allow to cool at least 15 minutes under the cloth. This will help assure the rolls stay soft even after they have cooled completely. Serve with clotted cream (if you can find it) and strawberry jam.

EZEKIEL BREAD

This loaf is loosely based on Ezekiel 4:9. It is our interpretation of the passage created at the request of numerous customers. The verse in part reads, "Take thou also unto thee wheat and barley and beans and lentils and millet and spelt and put them in one vessel and make thee bread thereof. We adapted our own version and came up with a great tasting loaf that is high in protein, low in carbohydrates, easy to digest and packed with vitamins and minerals.

2 Batch

Preheat to 400 degrees
Use dough hook

2 ¼	Tablespoon	barley (I prefer the cut variety but rolled will work fine)
5/8	Pound	flour, spelt
7/8	Pound	flour, bread
1/4	Ounce	salt
5/8	Ounce	yeast
1/4	Ounce	sesame seeds
2 1/4	Ounce	oats
1	Pound	great northern beans (canned, not dry - do not drain)
2 1/4	Tablespoon	olive oil
1/4	Cup	honey
4 5/8	Ounce	water

Mix all ingredients until you have a soft but smooth dough.

Allow to rise 1 hour in a warm place.

Divide into to roughly equal pieces and round. Let sit 10 minutes then roll into a short log to fit your loaf pans.

Place the logs in lightly sprayed or oiled loaf pans.

Allow to double.
Slash lengthwise down center leaving about 1 inch uncut on either end.

Bake in center of oven.

FARMHOUSE LOAF

This is a full sour dough modeled after some classic Italian country loaves. It is a large, four pound loaf in the traditional manner. It was usual for baking to be done twice a week on the large farm estates with enough bread being made to feed the family and staff throughout the week. If you have not got a sour started that you work with do so about four days prior to baking this bread. A simple one to yield enough for this recipe follows.

SOUR DOUGH STARTER
10 Ounce of bread flour
10 Ounce of water
Stir with a wooden spoon in a large bowl. Take a walk outside while stirring if you like to collect the wild yeast and sooth your spirit. Cover loosely with plastic wrap. Allow to sit in a warm place for two days. After two days add about three Ounce more flour and allow to ferment another forty eight hours. It is now ready for use in the recipe. You may keep any left over and just feed it a bit of flour every forty eight hours or so. You may need to add additional water at some point, enough to keep the entire sour about the texture of a soft dough. See section two for more detailed information on sour dough.

2 Batch
Preheat to 450 degrees
Use dough hook

1 1/3	Pound	sour
3 1/3	Pound	flour, bread
5 1/3	Ounce	flour, rye
2/3	Ounce	salt
3/8	Ounce	yeast
2 ½	Pound	water

Mix all ingredients until you have a soft, smooth dough. Approximately 12 to 15 minutes.

Allow to rise in bowl for one hour.

Divide into two roughly equal pieces and round. Dust the rounds with flour on all sides.

Let rounds rise until doubled. (About one hour)

When doubled, make 8 short slashes around outer edge and 1 small crescent in the center. Place directly on baking stone (preferred) or sprinkle a little coarse corn meal on a tray and place loaves on top of cornmeal. Fill the oven with steam.

Bake until dark brown, crispy crust and hollow sound when knocked.

FOREST MUSHROOM LOAF

This is an Austrian bread. I have never found a better bread for serving with beef, particularly a nice Prime Rib. It is great for sopping up juices the first time around and for making wonderful sandwiches the second time around.

2 Batch

Preheat to 425 degrees
Use dough hook

2	Pound	fresh mushrooms -- chopped
3 5/8	Ounce	butter, unsalted
7/8	Ounce	yeast
2 1/4	Pound	flour, bread
2	Tablespoon	molasses
7/8	Ounce	flour, buckwheat
½	Ounce	Brandy
½	Ounce	salt
7/8	Pound	water, from the mushrooms

Melt the butter, unsalted and saute the fresh mushrooms over high heat until they are cooked.

Drain the mushrooms reserving all the water. Squeeze them to remove all the water.

Put all ingredients except the water in mixing bowl and mix at 1st speed until you have a smooth dough. Add the mushroom water a bit at a time. You may not need it all depending on how dry the mushrooms are.

Allow to rise in bowl until doubled.

Divide into two roughly equal pieces and round. Allow to sit under a damp cloth until doubled.

Bake directly on oven stone until golden brown and knocks. About 40 minutes.

HERB BREAD

This is another Austrian favorite. It is one of those very forgiving breads that allows you to vary both the quantity and type of herbs to your own taste with no visible effect on the loaf. I love the chives, rosemary and sage listed here but many combination of herbs are possible. I would stick with dried herbs rather than fresh just because they can be chopped finer. This proved to be one of Lisa's very favorite breads and I would be in the dog house if I neglected to bring at least one loaf home on days that I baked this treat at the shop.

2 Batch

Preheat to 425 degrees
Use dough hook

1 1/8	Pound	flour, bread
5 2/3	Ounce	whole-wheat flour
5 2/3	Ounce	Sour dough (see section two)
1 1/8	Ounce	powdered milk
½	Ounce	olive oil
½	Ounce	salt
1/3	Ounce	yeast
3/4	Pound	water
1/8	Ounce	chives
		Rosemary to taste
		Sage to taste

Allow dough to double in bowl. About 1 ½ hours.

Divide into two roughly equal pieces and round. Allow to double.

Make one horizontal slash across the top of the loaf.

Place directly on baking stone to bake. Approximately 30 minutes

HONEY WHOLE WHEAT

This bread was unique in Spain. In old Europe whole grain bread was the staple of the peasants and lower classes because it was cheaper and easier to mill. Spain however had lots of windmills and so white flour was cheap and readily available to all and so a whole grain loaf was an exception and not a common one. This is a lovely whole grain loaf that even the kids can like.

2 Batch

2 7/8	Pound	flour, whole wheat
2/3	Ounce	salt
½	Ounce	yeast
2 3/4	Ounce	butter, unsalted
½	Cup	honey
3/4	Pound	milk
3/4	Pound	water

Preheat to 425 degrees
Use dough hook

Combine all ingredients except water in mixer bowl. Add water slowly until dough begins to come together. Turn speed up to medium and mix about seven minutes until you have a smooth, soft dough.

Allow to rise, covered in a warm place until doubled.

Divide dough into two roughly equal pieces and shape into a loose round and slightly flatten with the palm of your hand.

Allow to rise until doubled.

Using a meat thermometer or thick skewer poke five holes in the dough evenly spaced in a straight line. Poke two more holes in the opposite direction from the center hole of the first line. Push your skewer right through to the table in each hole.

Place directly on baking stone in center of the oven.

Bake until golden brown and sounds hollow when the bottom is knocked. Approximately 30 to 40 minutes.

KHACHAPURI

This fun cheese filled bread is from Georgia, no not our Georgia, the former Soviet Republic Georgia. It would traditionally use a sheep's milk cheese(s) but we found the combination listed below to be a great version. In some parts of the country these would be done as small individual cheese filled rolls. In other parts of the country the large version that we are so proud of is more usual. This is one of those items that I had to adapt the recipe with only a description and so when we had people from Georgia come into the shop and try it I was very pleased when they said, "It is just like back home!"

2 Batch

DOUGH

1 1/8	Ounce	yeast
1 1/8	Pound	flour, all-purpose
2 3/8	Teaspoon	salt
4 1/4	Ounce	butter, unsalted - room temperature
5/8	Pound	milk - room temperature

FILLING

1	Pound	Provolone cheese, shredded
1	Pound	Feta cheese, crumbled
2 1/8	Ounce	butter, unsalted -- softened
3	Each	egg -- beaten
1/4	Cup	coriander

Preheat to 350 degrees
Use dough hook and paddle attachment.

This is a soft dough using all-purpose flour so it is important not to over knead. You may not need all of the milk. The finished dough should have a soft, pizza dough feel to it.

Combine all ingredients and mix until you have a soft but not sticky dough. Set aside and cover to rise until doubled.

In mixer with paddle attachment combine all the filling ingredients. Mix on medium speed until they clump together in a single mass. Divide in two and shape each piece into a round ball and set aside.

Using hands or rolling pin flatten one dough piece into a circle about 10 inches in diameter. Place one cheese ball in center and fold dough up around it by pleating. Gather the tops of all pleats together and twist then slightly flatten to seal. Place loaf on parchment covered pan and allow to rise for 20 minutes. Repeat for second loaf.

Bake until golden brown and remove from oven. Allow to cool before cutting.

SICILIAN LOAF

Customer Joe Natoli shares my enthusiasm for good bread. He shared this recipe from his Grandmother's bakery in Sicily. Joe brought his enthusiasm and energy to the shop and worked with me to "get it right" before sharing the recipe. We had fun baking together and "got it right" with this great half whole grain, half white classic from Sicily.

2 Batch

7/8	Ounce	yeast
1 1/4	Pound	flour, whole wheat
1 1/4	Pound	flour, bread
1/3	Ounce	sugar
1/3	Ounce	salt
1	Ounce	olive oil
1 ½	Pound	water - approximate

Preheat to 500 degrees
Use dough hook

Blend all ingredients except water on first speed. Add enough water to get a firm but flexible dough. Mix on second speed about 6 minutes until smooth and satiny.

Allow to rise until doubled (about 1 hour)

Divide into two pieces. Shape them into a loose round and allow to rest 20 minutes.

Roll each piece into an even log about 3 hand widths wide, Grasp the outer two hand widths and squeeze between thumb and forefinger. You want to divide the loaf into three sections divided by a severe tightening where the sections meet. If you were to turn the outer sections upward the loaf would look like Mickey Mouse ears. Left straight this is called a "fish".

Allow to rise about 20 minutes

Glaze with egg whites beaten with a little warm water. Sprinkle well with sesame seed. Place glazed and seeded loaves directly on baking stone. Bake 15 minutes without opening door. Turn heat down to 425 and bake an additional 15 minutes without opening door. After this time check to see how they are doing , may need an additional 10 minutes or so of baking.

OATCAKES

These little jewels were probably our most popular "special" item in the shop. I like to think of them as the "lembas" of Tolkien's elves. They are actually a Canadian adaptation of an old Scottish recipe. They are tasty, healthy and virtually indestructible. They may get dry with age but retain their goodness for up to a month or more. They travel well and are filling so they are great for working in the fields as the farm hands of old used them or for taking on hikes and camping. Great for school lunches and mid afternoon office snacks they are versatile. Making them in large quantities at the shop was a bit of a chore because of all the hand work but smaller home batches are fun for everyone involved!

Traditionally lard is used but we made them with shortening at the shop though I personally prefer the lard version.

24 Batch
Preheat to 400 degrees
Use paddle attachment

1 1/8	Quarts	Rolled Oats
1 1/4	Pound	flour, bread
2/3	Pound	sugar
2 ½	Teaspoon	salt
1 1/3	Teaspoon	baking soda
2 1/8	Cup	Shortening or lard
½	Pound	water

Combine rolled oats, flour, sugar, salt and soda.

Work in lard or shortening as though for pastry then moisten with the water. Mix until it comes together into a single large mass.

Sprinkle some rolled oats onto the work surface. Place dough on top of the rolled and sprinkle more oats on top of the dough. Use your hand to flatten the dough and spread the oats evenly. Roll out dough to desired thickness (I usually aim for about 1/4 to ½ inch).

Using round cutter (size is your choice) cut out circles and set aside. Gather up any scraps and combine them by hand and roll out again using additional oats as needed. Repeat until all dough is used.

Place directly on baking stone and bake until golden brown (about 15 minutes).

A wooden pizza peel is great for placing the oatcakes but your hands will work just fine. Oatcakes will be soft and fragile when hot so remove from oven carefully. They will firm up as they cool and then be quite sturdy.

OATMEAL LOAF

The Scots say that oatmeal is the one food that is helpful to the brain and the whole body throughout childhood, adolescence and adulthood. They believe they have raised oats to the highest level and judging by this loaf they may well be right! This hearty bread is made from a "SPONGE" or mild sourdough. It also is swirled with a touch of cinnamon and brown sugar. A treat any time of the day! Try it toasted and drizzled with a bit of butter, unsalted and honey.

2 Batch
Preheat to 425 degrees
Use dough hook

For the sponge, stir the following ingredients by hand in suitable container and allow to sit at room temperature for about an hour.

4 3/4	Ounce	oatmeal - Steel cut
4 3/4	Ounce	flour, all-purpose
2	Tablespoon	brown sugar
½	Ounce	yeast
7 5/8	Ounce	water - body temp

For he dough combine the sponge and ingredients in mix bowl. Mix on medium speed until dough comes together in a smooth, spiral ball around the dough hook.

2	Ounce	powdered milk
2	Dashes	ginger
7/8	Teaspoon	salt
1 3/8	Ounce	butter, unsalted
1 3/8	Ounce	honey or maple syrup
1 1/8	Pound	flour, all-purpose
7 12	Ounce	water
		Swirl
1	Tablespoon	cinnamon
2	Ounce	brown sugar
	Glaze	
1	Ounce	butter, unsalted - melted

Allow to rise until doubled. About 1 ½ hours.

Divide into two roughly equal pieces. Using your hands flatten into a rectangle about 5 x 10 inches in size. Sprinkle with the cinnamon and brown sugar mixture leaving about 3/4 of inch around all edges. Roll jelly roll fashion and pinch and tuck the ends to seal. Place seam side down in a lightly sprayed loaf pan. Brush top with the melted butter, unsalted.

Allow to rise until about 1 inch above the sides of the pan.
Bake about 50 minutes. Knock to test doneness.

PAIN AU MAIS

This is a yeast raised corn bread. That alone would make it unique but it also uses frozen corn kernels to make it a truly neat addition to your collection of corn bread recipes. This is a slice-able bread that makes great sandwiches. Amazingly enough it makes a killer PB&J. Try it, you'll like it.

2 Batch

Preheat to 400 degrees
Use dough hook

3/4	Ounce	yeast
1	Each	egg
1 1/4	Pound	flour, bread
6 1/4	Ounce	cornmeal
2 1/8	Ounce	butter, unsalted - softened
1 1/8	Tablespoon	salt
2	Ounce	corn - frozen
3/4	Pound	water - body temperature

Mix all ingredients except corn kernels until smooth and elastic. Add corn kernels and knead just until evenly distributed.

Allow to double, covered (about 1 hour)

Divide into two roughly equal pieces. Shape into 8 inch rectangle about 3/4 inch thick. Starting from short end roll into a loaf shape and place seam side down in sprayed pan.

Allow to rise until about 1 inch above the sides of the pan.

Quickly cut two crosswise lines in surface of each loaf without deflating it.

Bake until golden brown and "knocks".

PAIN D'AIL

This French garlic bread is great because the garlic and butter, unsalted are roasted right into the dough itself. Try it with pasta or make a sandwich. The baking mellows the flavor of the garlic. From ancient Greece and Rome well into the Renaissance, garlic was the gift of love. During the middle ages it was given both fresh and in dishes on Valentines day. Who says you need to buy roses?

2 Batch

Preheat to 375 degrees
Use dough hook

1/3	Cup	garlic
2 1/8	Ounce	butter, unsalted - room temperature
1 2/3	Pound	flour, bread -- approximate
½	Ounce	yeast
1/3	Ounce	salt
½	Ounce	sugar
1/3	Cup	powdered milk
1 1/8	Pound	water

Process the garlic and butter, unsalted in a food processor until smooth.

Add all dry ingredients and part of the water to the mixing bowl. Mix on first speed until you have a shaggy dough mass that could be lifted. Add the garlic butter, unsalted. Add the remaining water if needed and mix on 1st speed until you have a soft, smooth dough that spirals around the hook.

Allow to double under cover.

Divide into two roughly equal pieces. Round and allow to relax for 10 minutes.

Flatten the rounds into a smooth oval. Fold in half lengthwise, pinch the seam together, tuck the ends, and place seam side down in lightly sprayed loaf pans.

Cover the dough with a slightly damp towel to rise. The dough should rise 1 inch above the rim of the pan.

Bake about 40 minutes until light brown and "knocks" (sounds hollow when tapped from beneath".

Turn loaves from pan onto a wire rack and allow to cool.

PAIN DE CAMPAGNE

"Bread of the country" This is the classic French bread. The Baguette was created in Vienna and the French adopted it with a passion un-equaled but it is the "Boule" that is the original French bread. Boulanger or "maker of rounds" is what the French call their Bakers of bread. We use a poolish made with whole wheat but it is more common to use rye. This is a great general purpose bread that can be broken for dipping or sliced for sandwiches. Crusty and hearty pair it with a good cheese and some fresh fruit and you have a meal!

2 Batch
The day before baking, make your poolish.

3/4	Pound	water
3/4	Pound	flour, Whole wheat
1/3	Ounce	yeast

Stir all ingredients together in a suitable container, cover and place in the refrigerator overnight.

Preheat to 450 degrees
Use the dough hook

The Dough

2 1/3	Pound	flour, bread
1	Ounce	salt
1 1/8	Pound	water

Combine all ingredients including the poolish that has been fermenting overnight in your mixer bowl. Mix on medium until it forms a smooth spiral around your dough hook (about 12 minutes).

Allow to rise for 1 hour.

Divide into two roughly equal pieces. Shape into loose round and allow to rise in a banneton, a towel lined wicker basket or on a counter. The basket or banneton will help it keep it's "round" shape a little better. Rising on a counter the bread will spread out a little flatter.

Allow to rise until doubled, about 1 hour.

Using a lame or a sharp knife make four slashes in the top like a tic-tac-toe board. Gently remove from basket and place directly on baking stone in the center of your oven.

Bake about 55 minutes until the loaf "knocks".

PAN DE PUEBLO

"Bread of the house" This is the quintessential every day bread in Spain. White, remember they had lots of windmills for milling, crusty and versatile. The crust is a bit thicker than baguette (but you can't do a proper baguette without injectable steam anyway) and the crumb a little lighter. I happen to like this bread a lot and would admit that it is one of my favorites.

2 Batch

Preheat to 450 degrees
Use dough hook

½	Ounce	yeast
1 5/8	Pound	flour, bread
1/4	Ounce	salt
5/8	Pound	water - body temperature
1	Each	egg white - for glazing

Mix all ingredients except the egg whit2 until you have a soft, pizza like dough about 9 minutes.

Coat the dough with olive oil and allow to rise until doubled. Punch down and allow to rise again.

Divide into two roughly equal pieces and allow to relax for 20 minutes.

Shaping - Flatten into oblong approx. 5 x 15 inches. Roll jelly roll fashion from the long side. Pinch the seam and ends to seal.

Place seam side down on a parchment or cornmeal covered tray. Make five diagonal slashes across the top. Take the egg white and mix it vigorously with one tablespoon of water then use this to glaze the loaf completely.

Allow to double again.

Place directly on baking stone in oven and place a bowl of ice on bottom of oven to create steam.

PANE alla CIOCCOLATA

Italians have made an art of using chocolate in unconventional ways. The trick with this bread is that it is not too sweet. Try it sliced with a little Marscapone cheese. You can serve it up with a cup of coffee are a fruity red wine. Try toasting twice and cutting into "sticks" to make a quick "Biscotti".

2 Batch

Preheat to 400 degrees
Use dough hook

½	Ounce	yeast
3/8	Teaspoon	sugar
1 1/8	Pound	flour, all-purpose
3 ½	Ounce	sugar
1/4	Cup	cocoa
1/4	Ounce	salt
1	Each	egg yolk
2 ½	Teaspoons	butter, unsalted -- room temperature
3/4	Cup	semisweet chocolate chips
5/8	Pound	water

Combine all ingredients except water just until blended. Add water a bit at a time until you have a soft dough. Turn mixer to medium and mix for two minutes.

Allow to rise until doubled, about 1 ½ hours.

Divide dough into two roughly equal pieces and shape into a loose round. Then cupping your hands gently press the round into an egg shape. Think Ostrich egg. Be careful not to tear the dough.

Cover loaves with a damp cloth and allow to double.

Place loaves directly on baking stone. After 15 minutes reduce oven to 375 degrees. Continue to bake until loaves "knock".

Be careful checking or removing the finished loaves as the chocolate chips retain heat and you can easily get burned. Use an oven mitt.

PANETTONE

The tall domed Panettone so common today did not appear until about 1921 when an industrial bakery started using it's own tall cylindrical forms for this bread. They caught on and by next Christmas many were using similar tall forms. The original Panettone is much older and was a shorter, round loaf baked either free form or in a spring form style pan. Some claim that the Milanese were so fond of bread they called all bread by the term of endearment *panett*. When a richer or larger bread was made it would naturally be called *panettone*.

I believe the tale told in a small village outside of Milan where a plaque stands telling of a skilled but poor baker named Tony who loved a women far above his station. She was in fact promised to a gentleman more suited to her status. The gentleman quickly realized she would never love him and in a great act of kindness sought out Tony and gave him money to buy the finest ingredients and said, "Bake your best for her." He did and *Panettone* became a hit and Tony's fortunes improved and her family relented and allowed the two lovers to marry. Baking is about passion so I have no doubts at all that this is the true origin of Panettone!

2 Batch

STARTER

1 1/2	Ounce	yeast
1 1/8	Ounce	water, body temperature
6 3/8	Ounce	flour, bread

Mix the starter by hand and leave at room temperature for at least two hours, preferably four.

Preheat to 400 degrees
Use dough hook

DOUGH

7	Each	egg yolk
½	Teaspoon	vanilla
1/4	Teaspoon	lemon extract
1/8	Ounce	salt
2 1/8	Ounce	sugar
3/4	Pound	flour, all-purpose
5 1/4	Ounce	butter, unsalted
2	Ounce	candied citrus peel
2	Ounce	raisins
2	Ounce	golden raisins

Glaze

1	Ounce	butter, unsalted -- melted

Put starter in mixer bowl. Add egg yolks, vanilla, lemon extract and sugar. Mix to blend.
Add half the flour and mix. Add the softened butter, unsalted chopped in small pieces and remaining flour until you have a smooth and elastic dough. Add the raisins and citrus peel and mix just until blended. YOU DO NOT WANT THE DOUGH TO CHANGE COLOR
Allow to rise until doubled (about 1 hour)
Divide roughly into two equal pieces. Shape into smooth balls and flatten slightly. Place in Panettone mold and brush with melted butter, unsalted. Cut an X on the top. Allow to rise until doubled. Place pans/molds in oven.
After 15 minuets slide them out and brush again with melted butter, unsalted. Turn heat down to 350. Bake until golden brown and skewer stuck in center comes out clean. Allow to cool.

PEASANT BREAD WITH FIGS & PINE NUTS

This is the oldest bread recipe I have in my collection. It is over 900 years old. It apparently came from a manuscript in a monastery in the Tyrol region, sometimes Italy, sometimes Germany. It is a basic peasant bread made with the coarse ground grains common to the poor folk of the time. It appears the monks would dress this version up with dried fruits and nuts for the Holy Days and distribute it to the poor. Rich or poor, this is a great loaf that has hundreds of ways to be enjoyed.

2 Batch

Preheat to 425 degrees
Use dough hook

1/4	Ounce	yeast
1/8	Ounce	sugar, brown
3	Tablespoon	olive oil
½	Ounce	salt
2	Ounce	rolled oats
3	Ounce	flour, rye
4	Ounce	flour, whole wheat
1 1/4	Pound	flour, bread
3/4	Cup	pine nuts
1	Cup	figs -- sliced
7/8	Pound	water

Combine all ingredients and mix on medium speed about 10 minutes. You want a firm, smooth dough that spirals around the hook.

Allow dough to rise, covered until doubled. About 1 hour.

Divide dough into two roughly equal pieces and shape into a loose round.

Allow the loaves to double.

Bake directly on baking stone in center of oven. Deep brown crust and "knock" for doneness. About 30 minutes.

PORTER CAKE

It is important to understand that Guinness Brewery created Porter Ale at the request of the Irish railroads. It seems they had reached the conclusion that they would not be able to stop their Porters from drinking on the job so they asked for a lighter version of the famous stout that was so popular. Some sharp baker created this "cake" using the Porter which some said was, "not fit for a proper Irishman to drink." The baker took it to a friend of his, a railway Porter who found the passengers loved it. Soon Porters throughout the rail system were telling their passengers that they new the best stops to get the cake and so it became enshrined as "Porter Cake". Some may question this tale but having traveled in Ireland I have no doubts at all.

2 Batch
Preheat to 375 degrees
Use paddle attachment.

6 3/8	Ounce	butter, unsalted
1 1/4	Pound	flour, bread
1 5/8	Cup	brown sugar -- packed
1	Cup	raisins
1 1/4	Cup	golden raisins
1	Cup	glace' or dried cherries (I love using dried Michigan cherries)
3/8	Cup	almonds, blanched
3/8	Cup	candied peel
4	Each	egg
3/8	Cup	Porter Ale - room temperature
3/4	Teaspoon	baking soda

Put the soda into the Porter, it will foam up so be certain you have a large enough container.

Combine the ale mixture with all other ingredients together with paddle until you have thick batter.

Divide the mixture into to round cake or spring form pans (9inch) and level.

Place a circle of parchment paper on top of the batter.

Bake until skewer comes out clean. About 40 minutes. The parchment paper will keep the top from getting to dark. Peel the paper off when the loaves have cooled slightly.

The first time I made this recipe I had just pulled the batch from the oven at the shop when I got the call that my dad was in the hospital and the family should be there. I grabbed one of the cakes and headed to Grand Rapids. The family loved the cake and though my dad never regained consciousness and died a few days later I know he would have loved the story of how '"Porter Cake" came to be.

PROVENCALE FOUGASSE

This cracker like snack is sometimes sold on street corners. Often it will be referred to as a "hand" as in "I'll take two hands, please." Large versions are sometimes called "Harps" or "Harp Fougasse" (All of these would be in French of course!) One of the great things about this little bread is that all manner of things can be used to season or flavor them lending them to being a perfect base to your own imagination.

12 Batch (approximately)

Preheat to 475 degrees
Use dough hook

3 ½	Pound	flour, bread
1 1/8	Ounce	salt
1 1/8	Ounce	yeast
5 5/8	Ounce	olive oil
1 7/8	Pound	water

Combine flour, water, salt and yeast in mixer bowl.
Knead on low speed until incorporated. Add the olive oil and knead for 10 minutes.

Add whatever flavorings being used in the last 3 minutes of mixing. See below for notes on flavorings.

Allow the dough to double in size. Scale into 5 ounce pieces.

Roll into ovals approximately 8 inches by 4 inches. Cover the ovals and allow to rise 1 hour. Flatten the ovals by hand until they are about half again as large.

With a sharp blade, cut five incisions **through** the dough. Three on one side and two on the other. Fill oven with steam. Stretch the openings slightly as you place them directly on the oven stone to bake. Bake until golden brown and crisp. About 15 minutes.

Flavor suggestions:
Shredded Parmesan is a good flavoring. Chives and crumbled crispy bacon works well. Cumin and diced onion. Herbs both fresh and dried, particularly Herbs de Provence Garlic, minced sun-dried tomatoes or minced jalapenos. You are limited only by your imagination and your taste buds.

PUGLIESE

The Puglia region of Italy is noted for it's almonds and this bread. The wood burning ovens of the areas bakeries use the almond shells in their fires imparting a unique flavor to this marvelous olive oil loaf. We may not be able to burn almond shells in our ovens but this is a wonderful version of this great bread. It's large size is needed to get the texture and crust just so. A neighbor was once reluctant to buy their first loaf because of the large size. They said, "There are only four of us to eat it and two are senior citizens who don't eat a lot." They sampled and decided to buy it anyway. Later that day when I got home they came over to tell me that they had all sat done with some tea and jam and the entire loaf was now gone.

This loaf will keep for a week easily and makes a great sandwich at any point.
1 Batch

Preheat to 425 degrees
Use dough hook

2 2/3	Pound	flour, bread
3/4/	Ounce	kosher salt
1	Ounce	yeast
1/4	Ounce	sugar
½	Cup	olive oil
1 1/4	Pound	water - approximate

Mix all ingredients and the water. Add additional water if needed a bit at a time to get a soft, but not sticky dough. The dough should hold it's shape. Knead on low until it becomes very smooth and elastic. (about 10 min) SHOULD BE SOFT BUT NOT STICKY

Cover and allow to rise until doubled. About 1 ½ hours.

Shape into a loose ball and allow to rest 10 minutes.

Gently pull the sides of the dough with the flat of your hands then tuck them underneath to make a neat, pillow-like loaf. Be very careful that you do not knead or punch down the dough or turn it over. GENTLE IS THE KEY.

Use your hands to rub a dusting of flour on each loaf and allow to rise until doubled, about 1 hour.

Lightly dust the loaf with flour again and place it directly on baking stone in center of oven, disturbing it as little as possible.

Bake about one hour until nicely browned and sounds hollow when "knocked"

PUMPKIN BREAD

A classic American favorite. Feel free to make it with or without the nuts.

2 Batch

Preheat to 375 degrees
Use paddle attachment

1 1/4	Pound	sugar
2 5/8	Ounce	oil
7/8	Pound	pumpkin
1	Pound	flour, all-purpose
1 5/8	Teaspoon	baking soda
1 1/2	Teaspoon	salt
7/8	Teaspoon	cinnamon
7/8	Teaspoon	clove
½	Teaspoon	baking powder
2 7/8	Ounce	walnuts
4 7/8	Ounce	water

Divide batter equally between two loaf pans that have been lightly sprayed or oiled.

Bake until skewer inserted I center comes out clean. About 60 minutes.

RYE (THE WORLD'S BEST)

This is a full bodied sour dough and will require the creation of a sour several days in advance of the baking. Once you have the sour you can keep feeding it and use as needed. This was modeled after a Rye I remember from my childhood. There was a Polish bakery on the west side of Grand Rapids that made wonderful breads including a great rye. The bakery has been sold several times now and the rye is not anywhere near what it once was but I was able to create this loaf that I think matches my memories exactly.

2 Batch
Preheat to 450 degrees
Use dough hook.

SOUR

4 ½	Ounce	goat milk
1/8	Ounce	old rye dough (will not be available until you make your first batch)
5 5/8	Ounce	water
1/3	Ounce	powdered milk
3 5/8	Ounce	flour, rye
3 5/8	Ounce	flour, clear

RYE SPONGE

5/8	Pound	water
½	Pound	rye sour
5/8	Pound	flour, rye
2/3	Ounce	yeast

DOUGH

1 5/8	Ounce	caraway seed
½	Pound	flour, rye
1 2/3	Pound	flour, clear
2/3	Ounce	salt
3/4	Pound	water
1 7/8	Pound	rye sponge (all of it)

MIXING THE SOUR
Place ingredients in sour bucket in order listed. Mix with paddle until oatmeal consistency. Cover and let sit 48 hours at room temperature. *Clear flour is a high protein flour that may be hard to find. A good quality bread flour can be used but if you can find Clear it is worth the effort. See section one for more details.*

MIXING THE SPONGE
Mix all the ingredients in a large container. Do not allow the mixture to be any warmer than 80 degrees F. Let the sponge sit covered over night until it has tripled in size and made a full drop.

Recipe continued on next page.

MIXING THE DOUGH

After the sponge has risen and then collapsed, it is ready to be mixed into the dough. Mix all the ingredients using 75 to 80 degree water. Mix on first speed until incorporated, then mix on second speed for 3 ½ minutes. DO NOT OVER MIX. The dough should be medium wet and slightly sticky.

FIRST RISING: Pull dough from mixer and let it rise on a floured tray, covered for 45 to 60 minutes.

Divide into two roughly equal pieces.

Round the loaves and let them relax on bench/counter top for 10 minutes.

Shape by hand into 4 inch by 10 inch loaves with squared off, not tapered ends. Press them into shape do not pound them into shape.

Place the loaves on trays that have been sprinkled with cornmeal. Cover them and let them rise until doubled. About 30 to 45 minutes. DO NOT OVER PROOF.

Glaze the loaves with a mixture of whole eggs beaten with milk (3 parts egg to 1 part milk). Lightly cut the loaves across the width starting at the bottom of one side, cut across the top and down to the bottom of the other side (use lame or razor blade). Start in the center and evenly space for a total of five cuts.

Fill oven with steam by placing a large bowl of ice on bottom of oven. Place the loaves directly on baking stone in the center of the oven. Bake for between 40 and 45 minutes. You are looking for a deep golden brown crust. "Knock" to confirm doneness.

SALT RISING

Salt rising does not have lots of salt in it. The name came from the way the sour was risen. In the old days of wood burning ovens, fuel was not cheap and so the ovens would not be allowed to burn all night. Among salts more interesting properties is the ability to retain heat. The Pioneers would heat a large pot of salt in the oven when it was in use during the day. They would then sit their bowl of "sour" on top of the salt which would keep it warm and fermenting highly over night. Thus the name "Salt Rising Bread". This is a recipe that we developed at the store so that we would not have to heat a bowl of salt.

2 Batch
Preheat to 400 degrees
use dough hook

Three days before baking - 1st Stage
2	Ounce	yeast
1 1/8	Ounce	whey or powdered milk
3/4	Pound	water

Two days before baking - 2nd Stage
To the first stage add:
7/8	Pound	flour, bread
6	Ounce	water, body temperature.

The day of baking - 3rd Stage
1 1/2	Ounce	sugar
½	Ounce	salt
2	Ounce	shortening
½	Ounce	yeast
1 1/8	Pound	flour, bread
2 3/4	Ounce	water

1st Stage
Mix yeast, whey and water in large container. Let sit in a very warm place for about 18 hours.
2nd Stage
Mix 1st stage with the bread flour and the body temperature water. Stir well and allow to rise in warm place overnight.
3rd Stage
Mix 2nd stage with sugar, salt, shortening, yeast, flour and water.
Mix 10minutes on medium. (This will be a real flimsy dough and not very fun to work with)
Rest 10 minutes then divide into two roughly equal pieces. Shape into loose rounds then roll gently into a log to fit your lightly sprayed/oiled loaf pans. You will be tempted to dust it with flour to keep it from sticking to you but resist the temptation. Use a dough knife and move quickly, it will work.
Allow to rise in the pans until about 1 1/2 inches above the rim of the pan.
Bake at 400 degrees until done (approx. 30 minutes)

SEED & NUT LOAF

German breads are most famous for their use of seeds and nuts. There are some recipes that have far more seeds and nuts then flour. Cucumber seeds are popular as well as flax, sesame, poppy, pumpkin and jut about any other you can think of. This is my version of this uniquely German style that proved to be very popular at the shop. Feel free to mix and match your own favorite seeds and nuts.

2 Batch

Preheat to 400 degrees
Use dough hook

1	Pound	flour, bread
4	Ounce	flour, whole-grain wheat
4	Ounce	flour, Spelt
2	Ounce	butter, unsalted
1/3	Ounce	salt
1/3	Ounce	brown sugar
1/3	Ounce	yeast
1/4	Cup	pecans
½	Cup	pine nuts
1/4	Cup	sesame seeds
1	Pound	water, approximate

Mix all ingredients except water. Add water a bit at a time until you have a smooth, soft dough.
Mix on medium speed about 8 minutes.

Allow dough to rise covered until doubled. About 1 hour.

Divide into two roughly equal pieces. Shape into a loose round and allow to rest 10 minutes.

Roll the rounds into a fat log to fit your lightly sprayed/oiled loaf pans.

Allow to rise in pans until about 1 inch above rim of pan.

Glaze with a wash of 1 egg mixed with 1 tablespoon of water.

Bake until done and crust is a deep brown.

SIMIT

Simit is a sesame ring from Turkey. Think of them as a replacement for the bagel. They are enjoyed at breakfast and for snacks through out the day. It is not unusual for Simit sellers to string the rings on a pole, heft it over their shoulders and sell them on the street corners or to wander through the large office buildings in the afternoon offering these delightful little treats.

12 Batch

Preheat to 400 degrees
Use dough hook

2 1/4	Ounce	yeast
1 1/8	Teaspoon	sugar
5 1/8	Pound	flour, all-purpose
1 7/8	Tablespoon	salt
2 ½	Pound	water

Equal parts dark molasses and hot water for dipping the Simit in.

A large pan of sesame seed for dipping the rings after the molasses wash.

Mix first 5 ingredients until you have a very smooth and springy dough, about 10 minutes.

Allow to rise until doubled.

Use your scale and cut into 10 ounce pieces. Round these into loose balls and allow to relax ten minutes.

Roll each ball into a 14 inch rope. Hold one end and twist the other. Form the twisted rope into a ring, pressing and overlapping the ends to seal. Place on a parchment covered tray or one lightly coated with coarse cornmeal to rise.

Dissolve the molasses in the hot water. Dip each Simit in the molasses water then in sesame seeds. Make sure the Simit is completely and thickly covered on all sides. Place back on trays

Allow the coated rings to rise about 15 minutes. Then rotate each ring in you hands until you have about a 7 inch circle. Put back on tray for 15 minutes.

When well puffed, gently put them directly on the baking stone in the center of the oven. Bake about 20 minutes until rich brown in color.

SOLDIER'S BREAD

The fortress at Louisbourg is one of the oldest castle structures in the new world. Built by the French in what is now part of the Cape Breton area of Canada the castle was one of the first to incorporate a bakery into it's design. The Bakery which was restored and remodeled several times still produces bread. The Soldier's Bread was the staple ration for the army, designed to be hearty and durable (it held up in the soldiers packs and is designed to be slow to soak up blood) this mixture of whole wheat and rye is leavened with a sponge starter. I am told this recipe dates to about 1729.

2 Batch
Preheat to 450 degrees
Use dough hook

1 5/8	Pound	water
1/4	Ounce	yeast
2/3	Pound	flour, rye
2 1/8	Pound	flour, whole wheat
1/8	Ounce	salt

The day before baking, make a sponge by mixing the water, the yeast and ½ of each of the flours together in a large container. Cover the container and let rise over night in a cool place.

The next day make the dough by putting the sponge and salt in the mixer with the dough hook. Add the remaining flour a bit at a time until you get a medium firm dough that is smooth and spirals around the dough hook. (About 10 minutes on medium speed)

Cover the dough and allow it to double. Punch the dough down and allow to double again.

Divide into two roughly equal pieces.

Shape into loose rounds and allow to rise in bannetons if you have them otherwise let them rise on a tray or counter.

Allow to rise at least 30 minutes.

Using a lame or sharp knife make an X slash across the top of each loaf.

Bake directly on baking stone in center of the oven for 20 minutes at 450 degrees. After 20 minutes reduce the heat to 350 degrees and bake until done, "knock" to test. (approximately another 40 minutes)

SOUR DOUGH ITALIAN

This is our own full bodied sour dough. It has a rich tangy flavor that is similar to a San Francisco sour dough. It will require that you have a well grown sour ready to use. I recommend that you place equal parts of good bread flour and body temperature water in a large container. Add a slice of peeled pear. Eat the rest of the pear. Gather your container and a large wooden spoon and take a walk in the woods or neighborhood while stirring the sour.

Allow the sour to sit for 48 hours. It should be bubbling and growing by then. Feed it with a little more bread flour and water to get it back to the original consistency then wait another 48 hours. Use the appropriate amount in this recipe and save the rest for future use. It can be fed regularly and will provide a great sour that can be used in many different recipes.

2 Batch
Preheat to 450 degrees
Use dough hook

5/8	Pound	Sour Starter
2	Pound	flour, bread
2 1/4	Ounce	olive oil
1/4	Ounce	salt
1/4	Ounce	yeast
1	Pound	water, approximately

Mix all ingredients on medium speed for 12 minutes

Cover and allow to rise for at least one hour.

Use a dough knife and divide the dough into two roughly equal pieces. Cut a walnut size piece and feed it to your sour for future use.

Round into smooth loose balls and dust entire ball with flour.

Allow to rise until doubled.

Make cross shaped slashes across top. Turn loaf 1/4 turn and repeat cross shaped slashes. You should now have an eight pointed star pattern cut into the surface of the loaf.

Place directly on the baking stone in the center of the oven. Place a bowl of ice on bottom of oven to create some steam.

Bake until done, test by "knock" , approximately 45 minutes.

SPELT (Whole grain)

Spelt is one of the oldest and most beneficial grains known to man. It is a water soluble protein which makes it easy to digest. It is a one of only a few vegetable proteins that has amino acids and it has long been seen as having healthful, healing properties. In our experience about 90% of people with wheat or gluten intolerance can handle Spelt. In the middle ages there was a German monastery that was noted for it's hospital. The monks used spelt in everything from their poultices to their meals. They treated their patients with some form of Spelt for just about every ailment that came to them and had a very good success record. Our friend and fellow baker, Fred Mesler helped us create this recipe. I don't know if this bread will keep you healthy but it is sure to keep you happy!

2 Batch

Preheat to 450 degrees

Use dough hook

The day before baking make a sponge as follows:

1 2/3	Pound	flour, whole Spelt
1 1/2	Ounce	yeast
7/8	Pound	water

Mix together until you have a smooth very firm dough. Cover and place in a cool place to rise over night.

The day of baking make the following dough;

1 1/3	Pound	flour, whole Spelt
3 5/8	Ounce	honey
7/8	Ounce	salt
2/3	Pound	water, body temperature

All the sponge made the day before.

Place the sponge in mixer bowl. Add other ingredients except water. Add water a bit at a time until you have a firm dough.

Knead on medium speed until you have a smooth dough that is spiraling around the hook.

Cover and allow to rise until doubled.

Divide into two roughly equal pieces. Shape into loose balls and allow to relax for 15 minutes.

Shape into a football or fat cigar shape by rolling gently on table.

Allow loaves to rise until doubled, about 40 minutes.

Make diagonal slit along the length half way between center and side. Brush slit only with salt water. Place loaves directly on baking stone in center of the oven. Bake about 1 hour.

STILTON & WALNUT LOAF

Over the years the English have taken some hard knocks for their cooking but nearly all agree that Stilton is probably the King of cheeses. This loaf combines Stilton with another product of the English countryside, walnuts. When cooking with cheese or wine you should always use the best that you can, after all, if you wouldn't eat or drink it by itself why would you want to put it in something special that you labored to create?

2 Batch

Preheat to 400 degrees
Use dough hook

3	Pound	flour, bread
2	Tablespoon	salt
2	Teaspoon	dry mustard
1 1/4	Ounce	yeast
1 1/2	Pound	water
5/8	Pound	Stilton
½	Pound	walnut
		milk for glazing

Mix all ingredients except cheese and walnuts to make a soft but not sticky dough. Cover and allow to double.

Divide the dough into two roughly equal pieces. Shape into loose rounds and allow to relax 15 minutes.

When relaxed roll or flatten the pieces into rectangles approximately 10 x 15 inches. Spread a layer of crumbled Stilton over them leaving about a one inch border all around. Top the Stilton with crumbled walnuts then roll up jelly roll style from the short end.

Tuck ends and place in well sprayed/oiled loaf pan.

ROLL TIGHTLY TO AVOID GAPS IN THE FINISHED LOAF

Brush the surface with plain milk and bake approximately 40 minutes.

STOLLE DE NOEL

This is our version of the classic Yuletide Stollen. This may well be the finest Holiday bread ever created and if I do say so myself, this is the best version of it I have ever had. Do not even think about using the word *"fruitcake"* . This delectable treat has no more resemblance to that "which must not be named" then an apple has to a fruit fly. *(Psst! I'll let you in on a Baker's secret. There are only 112 fruitcakes in the entire world and they just keep getting traded at Christmas.)* This is a bread that requires some effort and vigilance but rewards the baker in so many ways. Use the best ingredients you can afford and take your time.

2 Batch

Preheat to 350 degrees

use dough hook

The day before baking make the starter:

4	Ounce	flour, bread
3/8	Ounce	yeast
3/8	Cup	milk

The day of baking make the dough:

2	Ounce	sugar
1/4	Ounce	salt
1 1/3	Pound	flour, bread
3 1/4	Ounce	butter, unsalted
3	Teaspoon	brandy
1 1/8	Cup	milk
3/4	Cup	almonds, sliced
4	Tablespoon	currants
½	Cup	raisins
3/8	Cup	candied orange peel
3/8	Cup	candied lemon peel

Mix the ingredients for the starter with your dough hook until you have a soft, smooth dough. Place in a well covered container and place in your refrigerator over night.

Baking Day

Place starter in mixer bowl and add all other ingredients except fruit & nuts.

Mix on low speed until incorporated then on second speed for 7 minutes. Add fruit and nuts and mix on second speed for 5 minutes more.

Cover and allow to double (approximately 1 1/2 hours).

Divide the dough into two roughly equal pieces and shape into loose rounds. Allow the rounds to relax for 15 minutes.

Recipe continued on next page.

Roll each piece with a rolling pin to an oval approximately 10" x 8" thick.

Brush the surface with melted butter, unsalted.

Fold nearly in half the long way, leave about one inch of the lower edge projecting.

Cover and allow to rise for 1 hour.

Bake directly on baking stone in center of he oven for 45 minutes. Bake until a deep brown and "knock" for doneness.

Remove from oven when done and immediately brush entire surface with melted butter. It is important that this be done while the loaves are still hot. The butter will be absorbed into the pores that are open from the heat and keep the crust from getting hard even after it is fully cooled.

When fully cooled use a sieve to sprinkle entire loaf with powdered sugar.

Serve this warm or cold (I love warm). Try it for the holiday morning brunch or in the evening before the fire with a glass of Ruby Port or Grand Marnier. Wrap them in brightly colored cellophane with a jaunty ribbon and give them as gifts.! This is truly a holiday classic.

THREE GRAIN BREAD

This is a multi grain in the German style whose plethora of seeds and grains is exceeded only by it's rich flavor. I love this one toasted in the morning, spread with fresh butter and drizzled with honey. It is a breakfast that will keep you going throughout the day. This loaf's flavor is best when it has sat for a day and the rich flavors have melded into a complex and satisfying array. One customer swore that a thick slice of good Bavarian ham and German sweet mustard on this bread made the world's greatest sandwich! Try it for yourself.

2 Batch

Preheat to 450 degrees
Use dough hook

2	Pound	flour, bread
1	Pound	rye
2	Ounce	rolled oats
1	Ounce	salt
1	Ounce	yeast
½	Pound	milk
1 1/4	Pound	water

Flax seeds, for topping

Mix all ingredients except water. While mixing on low slowly add water to get a firm dough. Knead on low speed for about ten minutes or until you have a firm but smooth and elastic dough.

Cover and allow to rise one hour. Punch down and allow to rise one more hour.

Divide into two roughly equal pieces. Shape into loose rounds and allow to rest 10 minutes.

Shape the rounds into a smooth ovals with slightly pointed ends. I like to think of the shape as an upside down canoe.

Allow to rise in this shape until doubled.

Make a deep slash (½ to 3/4 inches deep) from pointed end to end.

Brush the entire loaf with milk and sprinkle liberally with flax seeds.

Bake directly on stone in center of the oven until done. About 40 minutes.

TUSCAN

Let me tell you a tale of a long time ago. In Tuscany about 200 years or so ago there lived a Prince who wished to build a new hunting lodge for his recreation needs. Not wanting to tighten his budget he decided to place a tax on salt to raise the needed funds. The people of Tuscany did not take kindly to another tax on something so vital (they thought) to their lives so they rebelled by giving up salt. After all you can't be taxed on something you don't use. This required adjusting a great number of heir recipes but perhaps the most difficult to adjust was bread. For not only does salt enhance flavors but it is essential to controlling the yeast who with out it would just knock themselves out in an orgy of reproductive bliss creating great empty balloons of crust. So these creative Tuscans came up with *"Bouillie"* which I am told means *"mush"*. By mixing boiling water with most of the flour for the bread and allowing it to sit overnight they could weaken the gluten structure of the dough so that when the yeast ran amok without salt to rein them in the structure would collapse and have to start over thereby avoiding having great empty shells of crust when the loaf was baked. A clever solution. Oh, yes, out tell of civil disobedience ends with most recipes from Tuscany be they soup, bread or what have you being salt free. Many till this very day. The end.

2 Batch
Preheat to 450 degrees
Use dough hook

The day before make the Bouillie;

2 2/3	Pound	flour, bread
1 2/3	Pound	water, boiling

The day of baking make the dough;

1 1/8	Ounce	yeast
2/3	Pound	flour, bread

For the Bouillie - Put the measured quantity of flour into a large container. Pour on the boiling water and let sit for 5 minutes. Then mix just to incorporate them. You should have what we like to call a "shaggy mass". Let the Bouillie rest, covered and out of drafts overnight.

The next day put the Bouillie and yeast in the mixing bowl. After mixing to incorporate them, add enough flour to make a medium wet dough. Mix for 14 minutes on medium speed.
Cover and allow to rise about 1 ½ to 2 hours.

Use your dough knife to divide into two roughly equal pieces. Shape each into a loose ball. And allow to rest, covered for 25 minutes..

Flatten the loaves slightly and fold edges to center sealing seams with flat of hand. Pull to slightly elongate and flip over. You want a nice pillow shape.
Allow to rise, covered for 30 minutes.

Bake directly on stone in center of he oven for about 45 minutes.

VIENNA LOAF

Vienna is a classic, rich, white bread that has been popular for centuries. A true Vienna will always have poppy seeds on the top but if you want you can leave them off. Just know that you will be breaking with centuries of tradition. I created this recipe by trying to duplicate another bread memory from my childhood. I don't know if my memory is off or if I am just really good at figuring things out but this bread matches my memory exactly. Imagine that!

2 Batch

Preheat to 425 degrees
Use dough hook

2 1/4	Pound	flour, bread
7/8	Ounce	salt
1 3/8	Ounce	sugar
1 3/8	Ounce	yeast
1 5/8	Ounce	powdered milk
5 1/3	Ounce	butter, room temperature
1	Pound	water

Mix all ingredients except the butter until you have a smooth dough that is spiraling around the hook, about 8 minutes. Add butter and mix just until blended in to the dough.

Cover and allow to rise one hour.

Using your dough knife divide into two roughly equal pieces. Shape into smooth, loose rounds and allow to rest for 10 minutes.

Roll the rounds into a Batard shape. Turn the loaf seam side up. Using a dowel or narrow rolling pin press a crease into the loaf right down to the work surface. Rocking the dowel will help keep it from sticking.

Turn the loaves crease side down onto a lightly floured surface. Allow to rise until doubled.

Turn crease side up, brush all except the crease with glaze of one egg mixed with one tablespoon of milk. Sprinkle the glazed area with poppy seeds.

Bake directly on stone in center of the oven. Bake until a mahogany brown and knock to test doneness.

SECTION FIVE

Humankind's struggle to reach beyond the known or *"Damn, this is good but what can we have with it?"* - Soups and creating a meal around bread.

Mr. & Mrs. Homeniuk had seven children. I'm the middle child. In a large family we all had chores to do and certainly some chores were routinely rotated among those of us old enough to perform them. Setting the table for dinner was one of these chores that rotated. If you set it last night you didn't have to set it tonight. A great system except that it left doing the dishes and sweeping the floor to also be rotated into.

My dad did not consider the table set if there was no bread placed on the table. This was not a function of the cook or even the menu. Bread was as integral as a plate or napkin to the table setting. Woe betide any who set the table and neglected the bread. This attitude was actually prevalent through out most of the world until relatively modern times. Indeed large parts of the world still build their meals around bread. In the United States we have come to think of bread as a side dish at best or something that is not even missed at worst.

Most cultures use bread as a central focus of their meals. A good, hearty loaf with that stew or fresh cheese to dress it up made a meal. Meat may be scarce or expensive, fruit out of season but with a good bread the meal can be complete with a considerably smaller portion than we tend to use in modern America. In short, meat, vegetables, fruit, cheese these were side dishes used to enhance the bread not the other way around as we tend to view them now.

You may have noticed that there is no baguette recipe in this cookbook. That is simply because without injectable steam and a stone deck you really can not make a proper baguette. I'll try and come close for the next cookbook. The point is that a baguette and some fresh fruit with a little cheese and good quality olives can make a great lunch or light dinner. A fresh baguette, a good goat cheese and some grapes are one of my daughter's favorite meals. The point I want to make is that there are advantages to changing your perspective from "What will this bread go with?" to "What will go well with this bread?" It is a subtle but powerful shift that can do wonders for your total calorie intake, balance and general health.

I will begin with a few of our customer's favorite soup recipes in this section and then start the wheels turning with some ideas to match up with the great home baked bread you worked so diligently to create. Some may seem obvious and others less so but don't be afraid to be creative with your food. Remember the poor schmuck who ate the first snail or sampled the first caviar.

I should note that long time customer and friend Ken Poff has an allergy to anything in the allium family, this includes garlic and onions. So "Ken Safe" soups became regulars on our menu at the shop on Tuesdays and the occasional other day. I have included some recipes here that are enhanced by adding onion and garlic and will note them as they show up.

A few soup basics;

There is no wrong way to make soup. Yes, you can substitute anything you like for any item in any recipe.

Some recipes may ask you to saute items before putting them in the stock. This will enhance the flavors of the soup. Not doing the saute will not ruin the soup by any means.

A hand blender or "stick" blender is a wonderful thing to have for working with many pureed type soups. It is a lot faster and neater than having to transfer hot stuff to a food processor.

You will always use less dry herbs than fresh herbs because the drying concentrates the flavors.

There are a number of advantages to having all things in a soup cut to approximately the same size. Cooking evenly and fitting in your mouth are just the two most important.

A soup pot should be heavy and thick. A heavy, porcelain lined pot for soup is a thing of joy.

A soup Tureen for serving at the table can make a simple meal something elegant. Treat your self!

When using dry beans be certain to plan to let them soak overnight. Un-soaked dry beans will never cook up to be as tender as soaked ones.

Canned beans are fast, easy and taste the same as dry beans when cooked in a soup.

Seasonings such as salt and pepper should always be added last in amounts that suit your taste.
This is what is meant by "correcting the seasoning".

Most soups become more flavorful when they are a day or two old. This is simply because the items in the soup have had time to mix and mingle and get to know each other.

Most soups will freeze well. Keep in mind that items such as potatoes or mushrooms that are porous and have a great deal of native moisture tend to turn to mush when frozen then thawed. This is because the freezing takes the moisture out and the thin membranes that held it in breakdown without the support. This usually has a greater effect on the texture then the flavor of a soup.
Making soup should be fun, creative and a great opportunity to have kids or friends help!

ADRIATIC POTATO SOUP

This was one of the soups that we opened with and it proved to be popular through out the years. I don't remember the original source that we used as a base but variations are found in many of the lands around the Adriatic.

6 Batch

5	Each	potato
1	Each	onion, large
2 1/4	Teaspoon	salt
2 1/4	Quart	water
3	Ounce	butter
2	Ounce	flour, all-purpose
1	Tablespoon	dill, dry
1	Pound	cream cheese
2	Tablespoon	parsley, fresh, chopped
1	Tablespoon	chives, fresh, chopped

Peel the potatoes and cut into large cubes. Peel and chop the onion.

Put the vegetables, salt, and water into soup pot and cook until potatoes are tender.

Melt the butter in a large skillet. Stir in the flour to make a roux.

Add to the soup pot stirring until the soup has thickened.

Add the dill and parsley and chives.

Break cream cheese into small bits and stir into the soup until melted.

Suggestions:
Try serving this soup with some of the Rye bread and a semi-tart apple such as a Honey Crisp. A green salad can round out the meal if it is kept simple.
Hot cider or a green tea make a nice beverage pairing.

ALSATIAN CHEESE SOUP

One of our "Ken Safe" soups. A good Gruyere cheese is best but even a basic factory produced Swiss will work. Grating the cheese helps it to melt faster but dicing it small will work. I use a food processor to grate and it saves a lot of time and effort.

6 Batch

3	Ounce	butter
4	Ounce	flour, all-purpose
1 ½	Quart	milk
1 ½	Cup	water
1 ½	Pint	Gruyere cheese, grated
3/8	Teaspoon	salt

Put milk and water in the soup pot and heat until just about to boil.

Melt the butter in a small pan and stir in the flour to make a roux. Whisk until smooth.

Add the roux to the soup and whisk until well thickened.

Stir in the cheese and salt.

Suggestions:
I like to add just a touch of black pepper.
Try serving it with a crusty bread like the Pain de Campagne or the Rye.
A plate of sliced cold sausage such as a nice Kielbasa or a Dry salami go well.
A bowl of assorted olives and a few fresh tomato slices drizzled with a flavored olive oil add zest.
A cold beer of your favorite variety would be in keeping with the tastes of Alsace.

BOGRACS GULYAS

This is a true Hungarian "Beef Goulash" or Bogracs Gulyas. We had a young woman named Noemi working at the shop for a time. Noemi was from Hungary and shared this recipe with us. I think it is best when the onions and peppers are chopped in large pieces. It became a customer favorite.

6 Batch

1/4	Cup	lard or shortening
2	Each	onions, large chopped coarsely
2	Each	green pepper, large, chopped coarsely
3	Cloves	garlic, chopped
3	Pound	beef, cubed
6	Ounce	tomato paste
1 ½	Pint	sour cream

Melt the at in the pot and brown the beef. Stir in all the other ingredients and allow to cook down. This will be a very thick "soup". Actually it is a "goulash" but who is being that picky.

Salt and pepper to taste.

Suggestions:
Serve it with the Pain D'Ail or Pain de Campagne or Pan de Pueblo.
A plate of cheeses such as Cotswold and Stilton would round things out well.
A sharp cheddar and a Taleggio would also be good choices.
Some thick cucumber slices, radishes and maybe some blanched asparagus would go well.
A mineral water or Piesporter would make a fine beverage choice.
Some apple pie for desert and everyone will say it was "good eating!"

BORSCHT

This is a Homeniuk family recipe that I remember my Grandmother and then my mother making. It was passed to everyone in the family. Borscht can be hot or cold, vegetarian or not but they all must have beets as the basis. Ours is a hot soup with a bit of pork in it. It has been a Homeniuk family favorite for several generations.

6 Batch

1	Pound	pork, steak
3	Quart	water
1	Cup	green beans, cut
1	Each	pickling spice ball
1	Each	onion, minced
2 2/3	Tablespoon	butter
2	Each	potatoes, peeled & diced
8	Each	beets, peeled & diced
6	Each	tomato, peeled, seeded & diced
1	Tablespoon	vinegar
1	Tablespoon	sugar
1	Cup	sour cream
1	Ounce	flour, all-purpose

Saute the onions in the butter. Add the meat including the bone and brown. Add the water. Fill a spice ball half full with "pickling spice" and add it to the water. Add the potatoes, beets, beans and tomatoes. Simmer until beets soften.

Add the vinegar and sugar.

Mix the flour with the sour cream until there are no lumps then add the mixture to the soup. Stir to blend.

Remove the spice ball and bone.

Suggestions:
Serve the soup with Black bread or Honey Whole Wheat or any of the multi grains
Serve a spinach salad with fresh strawberries.
A plate of pickles and maybe a few sardines or herring in a mustard sauce.
Cold vodka or Hot coffee are good beverage options

BROTCHAN FOLTCHEP

This is an old Irish recipe that is more than 1,400 years old. St. Colmcille is an Irish saint who was said to eat a bowl of this everyday of his life. There are older tales of Irish heroes who ate this everyday and reputedly lived to be nearly 200 years old. I make no claims but note that this soup contains ingredients that have been shown by modern science to be some of the healthiest items you can eat. Maybe the tales are all "Blarney" but it taste so good why take the chance?

6 Batch

2 1/4	Pound	leeks
1 1/2	Pint	vegetable broth or water
1 1/2	Pint	milk
3	Ounce	butter
1 1/2	Cup	rolled oats
3/8	Cup	cream
2	Tablespoon	parsley -- fresh

Wash the leeks well and cut into 1 inch pieces including the pale green leaves, set aside.

Put stock and milk into pot and bring to a boil.

Reduce heat add butter and allow to melt.

Add oats and stir well.

Bring to a boil add leeks and turn down to simmer for 20 minutes.

Add cream and parsley.

Season with salt and pepper to taste.

Suggestions:

Try serving this one with some Devonshire splits and honey or a little toasted Herb bread.
A good sheep's milk cheese such as Tomme du Berger from Corsica would make an excellent side.
Some crisp fall apples and a bowl of toasted nuts will fill out the meal.
A dark beer, a robust red wine or ice cold milk would be great beverage choices.

CASSOULET

Alright, I admit the Cassoulet is not usually a soup. This version however is a soup and falls so close to being a true Cassoulet that we kept the name. Cassoulet is one of the best known and most widespread of French dishes. Version are varied and multitudinous so why not a soup version? Unofficially, I think this proved to be our most popular soup of all time at the shop.

6 Batch

3	Each	onion (small) -- chopped coarsely
5/8	Pound	kielbasa, or any other garlicky sausage that you like, sliced
1	Tablespoon	thyme, fresh chopped well (½ tablespoon if you use dry)
2	Cup	white wine
1	Quart	chicken broth
2 3/4	Pound	great northern beans, canned
1	Quart	turkey, diced (Duck would be more traditional)
1/4	Cup	parsley, fresh, chopped well

Saute the onion and sausage in a pan over medium heat until onion is soft and sausage is lightly browned. Add the thyme and stir for one minute.

Add wine and boil until slightly reduced (about 2 minutes). Mix in the broth, half the beans and the turkey.

Puree the remaining beans and add to soup, stirring often, about 10 minutes. Season to taste with salt & Pepper.

Sprinkle parsley over the top and serve.

Suggestions:

Crusty bread is the key to this hearty supper. Pain de Campagne, Rye, Pan de Pueblo are all excellent choices.
Set out a plate of fresh figs and spiced olives.
A fresh goat cheese drizzled with a little Lavender honey would be appropriate.
A hard cider, strong tea, and any fruity red wine would be good beverage choices.
Try serving a basic apple tart to finish the meal.

Cheddar W/Ham & Jalapeno

This was one of earliest "Ken Safe" soups. It is popular with many of our customers whether they have allergies or not. It is a simple soup to make and lends itself readily to improvisations. Try it as is and then try it again making your own variations. I like switching the ham out for crisp bacon. It is also pretty tasty substituting shrimp for the ham. I like to garnish with a little chopped cilantro if I use shrimp.

6 Batch

1 3/4	Quart	milk
1 1/4	Pint	water
1 ½	Quart	cheddar cheese, shredded
½	Cup	jalapeno, finely chopped
1 1/4	Pound	ham, diced
1 3/4	Teaspoon	paprika
1 3/4	Teaspoon	salt
2 3/8	Ounce	butter
3 5/8	Ounce	flour, all-purpose, approximately

Put milk and water into soup pot and heat to near boil.

Make roux of butter and flour and stir into hot liquid. Heat and stir till thickened.

Add, cheese, stir until melted.

Add ham, jalapeno and spices. Stir well.

Suggestions:
Pugliese, Peasant w/figs and pine nuts and Sour dough Italian are great bread choices for this soup.
Any mixed green salad with a few toasted pecans will fill out the meal.
Serve warm chocolate chip cookies for dessert.
Mineral water, pilsner, or a sweet white wine to drink will work well.

Cream Of Tomato

This is a simple classic that beats the heck out of the red & white can variety. This lends itself to the ease of using canned tomatoes though fresh work well also.

6 Batch

1	Can	tomatoes, diced or whole
1	Cup	water
2	Teaspoon	chicken soup base
1 ½	Tablespoon	sugar (this helps delete the acid tang of the canned tomatoes)
3/4	Teaspoon	salt
3/4	Teaspoon	black pepper
2	Teaspoon	basil, fresh, minced (if using dry, 1 teaspoon)
1 ½	Ounce	Butter
½	Pint	Cream

Put all ingredients except basil, cream and butter in the soup pot.

Puree with the hand blender. (smooth but slightly chunky)

Add the basil and heat.

When hot add the cream slowly while stirring vigorously (the main thing is to not get too thin of a soup).

Add butter and allow to melt into the soup.

Suggestions:
The classic idea is to serve this with a grilled cheese sandwich. I recommend Swiss on Rye or Cheddar on Pugliese. Stilton on Pain de Campagne would also be nice.
A plate of carrot sticks, celery slices and a few artichoke hearts round it out.
Lemonade or fresh fruit juices should be the beverage of choice though on a cold day Hot chocolate goes surprisingly well with this meal.

Curried Pear

This soup came about from one of our cheese tastings. It proved to be popular and simple. Both of these traits are great in a soup. This is designed as a cold soup but it isn't too shabby hot!

6 Batch

3	Can	pears, large cans
2	Teaspoon	curry powder
½	Cup	water
1/4	Teaspoon	cinnamon
1	Cup	ice cubes
1 1/4	Cup	whipping cream
1	Each	Pears, fresh

Pour the canned pears with the juice into soup pot. Add the curry powder, water and cinnamon.

Puree with hand blender. Add ice cubes and cream and continue to puree until ice is broken up into small pieces.

Peel the fresh pears and then use your peeler to shave off thin slices into the soup. Use up both pears in this fashion.

Add a dash of salt to taste. Serve.

Suggestions:

Farmhouse loaf, Devonshire Splits and the Russian Black are all good bread choices for this soup.
A spinach salad with walnuts and a wedge of blue cheese add substance.
A chai style tea or iced guava juice make a refreshing beverage for this meal.
Serve a warm brownie or hot fudge sundae for desert.

Fiesta Chili

Hiring CJ Stott was one of the best decisions I ever made at the shop. He was responsible, a hard worker, fun (who can forget the Halloween that he dressed as a woman) and creative. He and I sometimes had informal Chili cook-offs to see who could make the most interesting chili. His Fiesta Chili proved to be a big hit with me and the customers. So without further adieu here is the Big Guy's Infamous Fiesta Chili!

6 Batch

5/8	Pound	hamburger
1/3	Can	green chilies (smaller than a tuna can)
1	Teaspoon	jalapeno, drained, diced
½	Each	Red or Yellow Bell Peppers, large
7/8	Teaspoon	cumin
1 1/3	Teaspoon	chili powder
1 3/4	Dash	coriander
½	Teaspoon	lemon pepper
7/8	Teaspoon	salt
1	Shot	tequila
1	Bottle	Corona Beer
1/3	Jar	Of your favorite salsa, hot
1	Can	Red kidney beans, large
2	Can	Tomatoes, diced

Place raw hamburger in soup pot. Warm to begin browning.

Add seasonings and peppers. Stir occasionally with spatula, chopping large pieces up with end of spatula.

If so desired, you can add 1 diced onion at this time, but you probably won't taste it.

Once meat is mostly browned, add Tequila. Once meat is thoroughly browned, add salsa and stir.

Then add tomatoes, beans, and enough beer to make soup. Let simmer for at least one hour before serving.

Suggestions:

The Mexican corn bread and the Pain au Mais are both excellent with this chili.

Serve it with a variety of pickled peppers on the side.

Your favorite beer, iced cold or apple cider make a great drink accompaniment.

Finish the meal with a large piece of dark chocolate!

GAZPACHO

This is my version of the Spanish classic. Additional vegetables can be added to suit your tastes. Radishes, cilantro, jicama, zucchini and asparagus are just some of the possibilities. Original to Andalucia, Spain there is a white version common to Malaga. Using grapes and almonds it has strong similarities to Moroccan bean and almond soup and may well stem from the days of the Moorish occupations of Spain. The traditional Gazpacho has become known throughout the world. Few do not love this "liquid salad".

6 Batch

3	Pound	tomato
1 ½	Pint	water, cold
1 ½	Each	cucumber, large
1 ½	Each	onion
1	Each	carrot
1 ½	Each	bell pepper
6	Ounce	crusty bread, day old at least
3/4	Cup	white wine, dry
1/3	Cup	tomato paste
3 1/4	Tablespoon	red wine vinegar
3 1/4	Tablespoon	garlic, chopped
2	Tablespoon	Red Hot sauce

Additional chopped -
  onion
  cucumber
  tomato
  green pepper

Puree first 12 ingredients in food processor in batches.

Strain through a sieve, pressing on solids with back of spoon. Cover and chill until very cold.

Chop remaining ingredients and mix in just before serving.

Garnish each bowl with spoonful of sour cream.

Suggestions:
Make croutons from a variety of left over breads and serve them with this soup.
Pick a firm strong cheese like a Manchego or Mahone as a side dish.
Close the meal with fresh figs and/or clementines drizzled with a local honey.
Sangria, Sherry or Limeade would be great beverages.

MOROCCAN BEAN & ALMOND

This is one of the more unusual soups we have run across. I have to thank a customer who was visiting from Morocco who told me about it. I never learned her name and she returned home soon after mentioning this soup. A little research soon found many variations so I created this adaptation.

6 Batch

3/4	Cup	white beans, canned
1	Quart	water
5	Ounce	almonds, blanched
3	Each	green onion, white part only
2	Clove	garlic
½	Teaspoon	salt
3/4	Cup	grape juice
3/4	Teaspoon	sugar
		white pepper to taste

Chop the green onion and garlic. Put into the soup pot with all other ingredients except the almonds.

Bring mixture to boil, reduce to simmer.

Add almonds and allow to simmer twenty minutes.

Season to taste with white pepper and additional salt if needed.

Suggestions:

Herb Bread, Oatcakes and Oatmeal bread all seem to go well with this soup.
I think that Khachapuri would really round out a meal.
You could serve some spiced couscous and dried dates on the side.
Fresh mint tea is always the Moroccan beverage of choice.
I would finish the meal with a lemon tart.

MULLIGATAWNY

This is actually a Scottish soup by way of India. In colonial days there were a number of Scottish regiments in India. They either modified a dish they found there or just used ingredients from India to create this once they returned home. There has been some scholarly debate over which it was. Most agree that while the soup has become popular in India it was probably made so by the Scottish regiments and was most likely not native to the region. So enjoy the soup with friends and have a conversation about the mysteries of it's origins!

6 Batch

2 ¼	Tablespoon	butter
1 ½	Tablespoon	flour
2	Each	tart apple (like a Granny Smith), peeled and chopped
½	Cup	onion, chopped
½	Cup	green pepper, chopped
1/4	Cup	carrot, chopped
2	Pound	chicken, diced
1 ½	Teaspoon	curry powder
2	Quart	chicken or vegetable stock
3/8	Cup	coconut flakes
3	Each	cloves, whole
2 1/4	Teaspoon	parsley
2 1/4	Teaspoon	sugar
1 ½	Teaspoon	salt
2	Each	tomato, peeled and chopped

Dredge the chopped apples in the flour. Melt the butter in a skillet and brown the apples.

Combine all other ingredients in soup pot and bring to a boil. Reduce heat and simmer for 15 minutes.

Add apples and simmer for 15 minutes more.

Suggestions:

Try this with some of the sweeter breads such as Cornish Saffron cake or a thick slice of pumpkin bread.
A plate of pickled beets, artichoke hearts and some Cotswold cheese would round it out nicely.
This would also be a good soup to serve with an Upper Peninsula pasty.
Use a dark chocolate cake for desert.
Tea, coffee and milk would all be good beverage choices.

ROASTED SQUASH, ONION & GARLIC SOUP

This takes a little time but is a wonderful cold weather soup. It keeps well and just gets better with a little aging. This is popular among my eighty nine year old in-laws and my daughter from the time she was five, so I would say it has wide appeal. Visit your local farmers market and look for some big heads of fresh garlic and a nice meaty squash.

6 Batch

1	Head	garlic, large and un-peeled
1	Each	butternut squash, large
1	Each	onion, large
2 ½	Tablespoon	olive oil
2 3/8	Teaspoon	thyme, fresh
5/8	Cup	cream, whipping
1	Pint	chicken stock

Cut 1/3 inch off top of garlic head exposing cloves. Cut the onion in half vertically. Cut the squash in half lengthwise and seed.

Arrange garlic, squash and onion cut side up on large pan. Drizzle vegetables with oil and sprinkle with thyme.
Cover with tin foil and bake until squash is tender (about 1hour).
Uncover and cool 15 minutes.

Scrape squash from skin into soup pot. Peel outer layer of onion and trim root end then add to pot. Squeeze garlic out of the cloves into the pot. Add any juices from bottom of pan. Add cream and use hand blender to puree until almost smooth.

Whisk in enough stock to get desired consistency. Stir over medium heat adding more stock if needed to thin. Season with salt and pepper.

Suggestions:

Pain D'Ail or Natoli's Sicilian are my breads of choice for this soup.
Use the bread for dipping or make a classic BLT to serve with the soup.
A classic quiche and a light salad could also round this meal out.
Hot spiced cider, Champaign or Earl Grey tea make great beverage options.
For desert serve up some vanilla ice cream topped with a fruit compote of your choice.

SOPA AL CUARTO DE HORA (Quick fish soup)

This is my version of a Spanish classic. Being a small shop I was often something of a one man band when it came to ordering supplies. As soups were done from scratch and in relatively small batches I found many an early morning where I did not have all the necessary ingredients for the soup that day. This is one of the ones that taught me that you can mix and match with what you have fairly easily and still please the customers!

6 Batch

5/8	Pound	clams, canned (weight is est. Use what is close based on whole cans)
3 5/8	Tablespoon	olive oil
2	Tablespoon	onion, minced (can be omitted)
1/3	Cup	ham, diced
2	Each	tomato, skinned & chopped
1	Dash	paprika
1	Quart	water
1	Cup	clam juice
3/4	Pound	cod
½	Pound	shrimp
2	Tablespoon	rice
1	Tablespoon	parsley, minced
1	Each	egg, hard boiled
		salt and pepper to taste

Chop the clams if whole.

Place all ingredients but parsley and egg into the pot. Bring to boil and reduce to simmer for 8 minutes.
You can boil the egg ahead of time or just slip it into the pot when it is coming to a boil. Fish it out when it has had time to cook.

Shell the egg and chop it. Mix with the parsley and add to the pot just before serving.

Suggestions:

Just about any bread you like will work well with this versatile soup.
I would probably pick a bread to go with a soft cheese such as a Bucheron, Camembert or an Epoisses to serve along side the soup.
A fresh fruit plate would also work well.
A Chardonnay or Rhine would be good drinking.
For desert try a slice of Brioche topped with mixed fresh berries and drizzled with honey.

SOYER'S SOUP

Soyer was a member of Britain's parliament who had large holding's in Ireland. He was known to be cheap and less then kind to the peasants that worked his Irish holdings. He begrudged spending money to feed his vassals and so took to having the kitchen make a soup from what would otherwise have been thrown to the pigs. The peasants took exception and began an up-rising based on English law that said a "Lord Holder" had to treat his vassals humanely. The crown was not happy with the uprising but Soyer had a pot of the soup made to be tested by parliament. In 1847 the British parliament ruled that *"...having been tasted by numerous nobleman members of parliament and several ladies of good standing who suffered no ill effects we consider it good and nourishing for the Irish peasantry"* And so Soyer was found not guilty of mis-treating his peasantry. The up-rising was declared illegal and put down ruthlessly. The soup as adapted here is tasty but I am certain we are using a little better ingredients then the Irish were allowed in 1847.

6 Batch

1 ½	Each	onion (original was onion peel)
6	Ounce	flour, all-purpose
3	Ounce	beef (original called for meat no longer useable by his lordship's staff)
1	Bunch	celery tops
1	Bunch	leek tops
2	Each	turnip peelings
6	Ounce	pearl barley (original called for barley from the stable supply)
1 ½	Gallon	water
3/4	Ounce	bacon drippings
		salt and pepper

Fry the chopped onions and diced beef in the drippings. Add the finely cut vegetables. Stir over a low fire for 10 minutes more. Mix in the flour and the barley. Add the water and simmer for 3 hours.

Suggestions:

Serve with Pain de Campagne or any of the whole grain loaves.
Large deli pickles and a chunk of sharp cheddar will dress this up more than the Irish were allowed.
Some smoked salmon will round out the meal.
Serve a cold beer or cider and drink a little humble pie for we all have things in our past that we should not be proud of.

SPANISH VEGETABLE

This is a basic vegetable soup with a Spanish take. I found myself enjoying vegetable soups of all kinds after trying this one. I don't know if my tastes were just changing of if this had that large of an impact on me. I am willing to bet that you'll love this one even if you are not fond of vegetable soups!

6 Batch

1 ½	Each	onion, med
2	Each	potato
½	Cup	olive oil
1 ½	Quart	water
3	Each	carrot, diced
½	Pound	green beans, cut
½	Pound	spinach
1 ½	Each	green pepper
1 7/8	Tablespoon	garlic, minced
3/8	Teaspoon	salt
1 1/8	Teaspoon	cumin
3/4	Teaspoon	basil
3	Tablespoon	parsley
2	Each	egg yolk, hard boiled

Peel and chop the onions. Peel and dice the potatoes. In a soup kettle saute both until brown in the olive oil. Add carrots and green beans.

Chop the spinach. Dice the green pepper add everything except egg yolk to kettle.

Beat the egg yolks with a little water to make a paste. Stir into the soup.

Simmer 10 minutes.
Serve hot.

Suggestions:

The Ezekiel bread or Spelt will make this a very healthy meal.
Serve a little tapenade and some hard boiled eggs on the side.
A fresh fruit salad with plenty of citrus is one way to go.
If you can find Spanish Tetillia cheese that would be great. This mild semi-soft cheese has a fun history that can be guessed at by it's name and would be a great addition to a meal built around this soup.
Fresh squeezed lemonade or limeade would be a good drink choice.

SPICY RED LENTIL

This variation on a Turkish soup came from Sema who attended school at MSU during our early days and discovered she liked what we did. Sema returned to Turkey but we kept the recipe!

6 Batch

7/8	Cup	lentils, red
3	Ounce	tomato paste
1 1/4	Ounce	butter
5/8	Cup	flour, all-purpose
1 1/4	Teaspoon	salt
2 3/8	Teaspoon	pepper
1/3	Teaspoon	paprika
1 1/4	Dashes	cayenne
		water

Boil the lentils in ½ gallon of water until soft.

Make a roux with the butter and flour. Add 3 cups of water and the tomato paste to the roux.

Whisk the roux and tomato mixture into the lentils.

Stir until well mixed. Add seasonings and water if needed.

Bring to a simmer for 15 minutes.

Suggestions:

Simit of course would be the first choice as they are also Turkish and the sesame would add a nice flavor to the mixture. Provencale Fougasse would also be very good.
A selection of dried fruits and olives would be a great side.
Slices of cold roast lamb garnished with lemon would be tasty.
Mint tea or strong coffee would make good beverage choices.
A selection of baklava would be a great finish.

VICHYSSOISE

This is one of life's great gifts. A good vichyssoise is some of the finest dining I have ever enjoyed. It must be made a day ahead of serving so that it can be properly chilled. There are some purist out there who say that it must be served at precisely 52 degrees. I don't think you need to be that precise but it does need to be refrigerated over night before serving. To call this cold potato soup would be doing a great injustice to any who had never tried it.

6 Batch

1 1/2	Each	onion, medium, chopped
5	Each	leeks, white part only
1/4	Cup	butter
4	Each	potato, peeled and chopped
2	Pint	chicken or vegetable stock
2 1/4	Teaspoon	salt
1 1/2	Cup	milk
1	Pint	cream
		chives

Put all except milk and cream in pot and heat to a boil. Cook until the vegetables are very tender.

Use hand blender to puree in pot. Add cream, thin further with milk only if needed.

Place in refrigerator over night to chill.

Sprinkle fresh chopped chives on top of each bowl when serving.

Suggestions:

This soup is rich and wonderful by itself. I admit I do enjoy it with a roast beef sandwich, cold or a classic French dip with au jus.
A green salad with chicken and toasted walnuts and almonds would work well.
The dressing should be light so as not to overwhelm the flavors of the soup.
You could try serving some Pan de Pueblo with a little smoked whitefish along side this soup.

ZOLDBAB LEVES

This is another recipe from Noemi the young woman from Hungary who worked at the shop for a time. It is a simple recipe but one that I really like. I am not certain it was ever a big seller at the shop but what is the point of being the boss if you can't occasionally make soups that you like!?

6 Batch

1 2/3	Quart	water
3	Tablespoon	chicken soup base
1 1/2	Pound	green beans, cut
1 1/2	Cup	onion, diced
1/4	Cup	butter
1 1/2	Teaspoon	paprika
1/4	Cup	flour, all-purpose
1/4	Cup	vinegar
3/8	Cup	parsley
1 1/2	Cup	thin noodles

Place all ingredients except the noodles and parsley into the pot. Bring to a boil and reduce to a simmer for 15 minutes.

Add the noodles and parsley.

Simmer for 10 minutes more. Serve.

Suggestions:

I like the Farmhouse loaf or any other full bodied sour dough with this soup.
This one lends itself to a platter of cold cuts and cheese. I would use some farmers ham, roast beef and maybe a dry salami for the meats. A nice Comte' or a Jarlsberg along with a sharp cheddar like Mrs. Quick's would be nice for the cheeses.
A hearty beer or chilled Aquavit would be appropriate to drink. Tea or fruit juice would also be good.
For dessert, a cherry strudel or tart would bring the meal to a first class end.

SECTION SIX

Enhancing taste not covering it up or *"What do you think will happen if we mix this and that?"* - Spreads, butters and sundries.

Good bread can stand on it's own but it also can become something more with a little enhancement. How many of us have not enjoyed a piece of toast with a little butter and homemade preserves. When was the last time you ate at an Italian restaurant and did not get a bowl of flavored olive oil to dip bread into? Lets cover some basics and then add a few recipes for you to try.

Making an infused olive oil is easy enough. Buy a good grade of olive oil. If you are going for mild flavor use an extra virgin oil. If you want a heartier flavor go with a cold press or blend. Pick your oil and a clean bottle. Warm the oil just slightly above body temperature and put your flavoring into the warm oil. Let it cool and sit for about 24 hours. Then strain the oil into your clean bottle and label what it is. Simple as that!

Some flavor possibilities are listed next starting with herbs. By the way fresh is best for this sort of thing but dry herbs will work also. In the herb category you might try, Rosemary, Thyme, Lavender, Chive, Garlic, Lemon Balm, Bergamot, Juniper, Fennel, Dill, Bay, Peppermint, and Cinnamon to name a just a few.

Some truly excellent oils can be made with peppers of various kinds though I recommend not mixing varieties of peppers. Do a batch of Chili oil and a batch of Sweet Bell but don't try combining them. Many nuts lend themselves to their own oils, such as walnut oil or almond oil. You can also use walnuts or almonds to flavor your own oils.

Remember with infused oils for dipping bread you are looking for hints and nuances of flavor, not overwhelming, pound the taste buds flavors. This is also why you want to strain your oils after 24 hours because they can quite often become bitter as the herb or flavoring item begins to break down.

Butter is hard to beat on warm bread but it can be varied. Remember all those herbs we mentioned above. Chop them fine and blend in with some softened butter to make an herb butter. Honey by itself or blended into a butter can be a wonderful thing to spread on bread. Shop for local honeys. They have some benefit if you have allergies but they also offer a variety of flavors based on what the bees were feeding on. The big commercial honey producers are usually blending honeys from many countries and so they start to taste all the same. You can also flavor your honey. Add a little Lavender as though you were infusing an oil. Use a little lemon extract to sharpen a favorite honey. Cinnamon can be easily added to honey either as ground cinnamon or as an essential oil.

There are some wonderful Jams, Jellies and Preserves out there in a plethora of flavors. Making your own is always an option. There are a lot of good books with recipes out there for Jams, Jellies and Preserves. I will share with you the difference between these three things. Jellies are made only from the juice of the fruit. Jams are made only from the solid parts of the fruit. Preserves are made from the entire fruit.

Now, lets look at some more unusual spreads.

AVOCADO GOAT SPREAD

Peel & pit an avocado.
Place in a bowl and mash until smooth.
Add about 5 Ounce of soft goat cheese, 1 teaspoon of olive oil (pick a good one)
Add 1 tablespoon of lemon juice.
Add a touch of freshly ground pepper and mash it all together until smooth.

RICOTTA & FIG SPREAD

Take about 3 Ounce of good ricotta, drain it well.
Steam & peel 2 or 3 fresh, ripe figs.
Mash the figs well and blend with the ricotta add just a touch of honey.

CURRY SPREAD

Combine 1 cup of mayo with 1 ½ teaspoon curry powder.
Add ½ teaspoon dry mustard, 1/4 teaspoon salt & 2 teaspoons lemon juice.
Blend until smooth.

AVOCADO BUTTER

Process 1 avocado and 1 pound of softened butter.
Add 1/4 cup lemon juice, process until smooth.

ATO SAUCE (African Red Sauce)

Combine in a processor:
1/4 cup dry red wine with 1 tsp ground red pepper, 3/4 tsp salt, 1/4 tsp ginger, 1/8 tsp cardamom, 1 clove garlic, 1/8 tsp coriander, 1/8 tsp nutmeg, 1/8 tsp cloves, & 1/8 tsp cinnamon.
Blend well.
Heat 1/4 cup of paprika in a sauce pan and add the pepper mixture.

When well blended and heated through mix just 2 tablespoons with your choice of 1 cup bottled chili sauce, mayo, butter or cream cheese. (Experiment with other ideas)

A little of the pepper paste goes a long way. The leftover paste keeps well in the refrigerator and can be used later.

APPLE NUT SPREAD

2	Tablespoon	Cream sherry
4 ½	Cup	Apples, peeled & sliced
1/3	Cup	Dates, pitted
½	Cup	Cottage cheese
1/4	Cup	Cream
½	Teaspoon	Cinnamon
2	Tablespoon	Almonds, slivered & toasted

Cook apples and dates in sherry until soft.
Place in processor with other ingredients **except almonds**.
Blend until smooth.
Stir in almonds by hand.
Cover and chill.

TAPENADE

Nearly every culture of the Mediterranean has tapenade. The recipes vary greatly. When I first went looking for recipes I found over 200 in no time at all. Some were as diverse to include figs or pistachios or oranges. The two things that are traditionally included are Kalamata olives and anchovies. We strayed from tradition at the shop by eliminating the anchovies. It is a wonderful spread and is extremely versatile. On more than one occasion my daughter and I have made a meal of baguette slices spread with tapenade. Here is our recipe (it makes a pretty large batch).

1 3/4	Pound	olives, Kalamata, pitted and chopped
2	Head	garlic, minced
1 1/4	Cup	olive oil
1	Each	lemon, juice
3/4	Cup	Thyme, fresh
2	Teaspoon	pepper

In a processor, chop olives, thyme & garlic together to coarse texture.
Add olive oil, lemon juice and pepper.
Seal tightly and refrigerate.
Best when allowed t o marinate for at least six hours before using.

ALMOND BUTTER

2.5	Pound	Almonds. toasted
3	Ounce	Peanut oil
		salt, to taste

Toast almonds in cast iron pan on top of stove. Shake frequently to brown all over. A little oil can help. Place in food processor and process a couple of minutes. Scrape sides of bowl and process until forms a thick paste. Add salt to taste. Store covered tightly.

CASHEW BUTTER

2.5	Pound	Cashews, toasted
3	Ounce	Peanut oil
		salt, to taste

Toast cashews in cast iron pan on top of stove. Shake frequently to brown all over. A little oil can help. Place in food processor and process a couple of minutes. Scrape sides of bowl and process until forms a thick paste. Add salt to taste. Store covered tightly.

HAZELNUT BUTTER

2.5	Pound	Hazelnuts, toasted
3	ounce	Peanut oil
		salt, to taste

Toast hazelnuts in cast iron pan on top of stove. Shake frequently to brown all over. A little oil can help. Place in food processor and process a couple of minutes. Scrape sides of bowl and process until forms a thick paste. May need some additional oil. Add salt to taste. Store covered tightly.

STILTON BUTTER

1	Pound	Stilton, room temperature
1	Pound	Cream cheese, room temperature
1	Pound	Butter, room temperature
1/4	Cup	Cognac

Using mixer or food processor cream all ingredients together until fluffy.
Serve at room temperature.
This makes a big batch but it is so tasty it tends to disappear quickly.

MAYO

Here is a basic mayo recipe for those of you who prefer not to have the chemical additives so common in commercial brands.

4	Each	Egg Yolks
½	Teaspoon	Mustard
½	Teaspoon	Salt
1 1/4	Cup	Oil, Safflower
1 1/4	Cup	Oil, Olive
1/4	Cup	Lemon Juice
½	Tablespoon	Lemon Zest

Have all ingredients at room temperature.
Place yolks, mustard, salt and lemon zest in processor. Process until pale yellow and foamy. Pour half the oil slowly through tube while processing. When it begins to thicken alternate lemon juice and remaining oil until fully blended.

Store tightly covered in refrigerator.

ZESTY MARINATED OLIVES

3/4	Quart	Olives, Kalamata, washed and drained
3/4	Quart	Olives, green cracked, washed and drained
½	Quart	Olive oil
½	Cup	Cilantro, fresh
½	Cup	Lime juice
½	Cup	Orange juice
1/4	Cup	Garlic, chopped
1/4	Cup	Parsley, chopped
2	Tablespoon	Lemon zest
2	Tablespoon	Orange zest
1	Teaspoon	Red pepper flakes

Combine all ingredients in a container. Seal tightly and refrigerate 2 days.

Should be served room temperature.

SECTION SEVEN

Man does not live by bread alone or *"I didn't know you could do that with chocolate!?"* - Desserts and other sweet treats

At the International Bread Company we made our reputation on recreating, traditional breads from many parts of the world. In truth we had over 170 breads in our line-up, representing more than 60 countries. We did however make some killer sweets also.

I have included a few of our customer favorites in this section. Details are provided with the recipes but a few universal notes are included here.

The number one complaint people have about their cheese cakes is cracking. There are two simple reasons why cheesecakes crack. The first addresses the concentric cracks that sometimes occur. You know those cracks that seem to follow the sides of the pan in big or little half moons. These occur because after the eggs were added to the batter they were beaten to long. You can beat the batter prior to the eggs as long as you like with little if any harm to the finished cheesecake. Once the eggs are introduced you want to mix only until they are incorporated and no longer. The second and more common cracks are the large, straight Grand Canyon cracks that run right across the cheesecake. These are caused by **over baking!** You most over come the notion that if the middle is still wiggly it is not done! The cheesecake is designed to be wiggly in the center when it comes out of the oven. What you should be looking for is the edges to be puffing slightly and rounding over. This is when the cake is done and when it should be removed. The center will set up just fine as it cools and refrigerates overnight.

It is always worth spending the little more to buy the good chocolate, always! There are many grades and brands of chocolate available. In the greater scheme of things your chocolate purchases are not a huge part of your budget. Buy the good stuff! It really is better.

Remember, most people you will be serving new treats to do not know how they are supposed to look. So as a very talented pastry chef once told me, "There are never any mistakes. If things don't turn out exactly the way I intended I just tell people I used the Viennese method. They don't know how it should be and enjoy it just as much no matter what I may think of it's appearance." These are good words to remember. We are usually our own worst critics. So don't be so hard on yourself!

The occasional treat is not going to harm anyone's health or diet. So don't go berating yourself saying "I really shouldn't make this cake." The moral boost alone is worth more than any calories it may have. Should you have one everyday, of course not. Should you have one know and again the answer is a resounding yes. Health and diet gain more from moderation in all things then they do by enforced deprivation. So don't be afraid to enjoy and indulge. People have been doing it for years and there are more people living longer than ever before on this planet. Use some sense and enjoy the taste sensations that life has to offer!

CINNAMON ROLLS

These are the rolls I remember my Grandmother making though I never had the recipe. They had a very loyal following of morning customers because they are not frosted. Warm from the oven is great but they do freeze well also. Thaw them at room temperature and then wrap them in foil and place them in a preheated (450 degrees) oven for about 10 minutes until they are warmed through.

12 Batch

Preheat to 375 degrees
Use dough hook
Allow dough to rise overnight before making the rolls

3	Pound	flour, all-purpose
2	Ounce	yeast
3/4	Cup	sugar
3/4	Cup	milk, powdered
1/8	Ounce	salt
3/4	Teaspoon	cinnamon
1 1/4	Pound	water
½	Cup	oil, vegetable
	Filling	
½	Pound	butter, room temperature
1/4	Cup	cinnamon,
1 1/2	Cup	sugar, brown

In mixer bowl blend together the flour, yeast, sugar, milk powder, salt and 3/4 teaspoon cinnamon. Add the water and oil.

Mix for 5 minutes on 1st speed. Add additional flour if needed to get smooth , malleable but moist dough.

Place in a covered container and allow to rise in refrigerator overnight.

Roll to large rectangle on work surface. Spread butter over dough. Sprinkle with cinnamon then brown sugar. Roll jelly roll fashion.

Cut into approx. 2 inch thick pieces. place about one inch apart on lightly sprayed or oiled baking sheet.

Let rise for 20 minutes.

Bake for about 20 minutes until rolls are golden brown.

CHOCOLATE CHIP COOKIE

Our chocolate chip cookies were always a hit. I think the biggest reason was that we included plenty of chocolate chips. We made a large batch of batter at the beginning of the week and just scooped and baked as needed throughout the week. The dough refrigerates well and so you can have fresh warm cookies in minutes if you choose to make a large batch of dough.
The kids and spouses will love coming home to warm cookies.

12 Batch

Preheat to 400 degrees
Use paddle attachment

3 1/3	Ounce	butter
2 2/3	Ounce	shortening
1	Cup	brown sugar, packed
½	Cup	granulated sugar
2	Each	egg
2	Teaspoon	vanilla
1 ½	Pint	flour, all-purpose
1	Teaspoon	baking soda
½	Teaspoon	salt
1 ½	Pound	chocolate chips

Beat butter, shortening and sugars until light and fluffy.

Add egg and vanilla, beat very well. (10 minutes on high)

Stir together dry ingredients then slowly blend into butter mixture.

Stir in chocolate chips and bake as needed. *(An ice cream scoop makes a nice size cookie.)*
Just evenly place the balls of dough on an un-greased baking sheet and pop in the oven.

CHOCOLATE HEART ATTACK

I won a bronze medal in my first Chocolate competition with this little treat. I thought it was pretty good for the first time competing by a guy whose skill was in breads. Friends, family and customers liked it too and it became one of our best sellers in the shop.

1 Batch
Preheat to 375 degrees

3/4	Pound	semisweet chocolate, coarsely chopped
4	Ounce	unsweetened chocolate, chopped
1	Pound	butter
1	Cup	brown sugar, packed
8	Each	eggs
1	Pinch	cayenne pepper
½	Cup	Kirsch (you can substitute Grand Marnier for variety)

Line the bottom of a 9 inch diameter by 2 inch high cake pan with parchment paper.

Place all chocolate in a large bowl. Bring butter and sugar to boil in sauce pan.

Stir until sugar dissolves. Remove from heat and pour into bowl with the chocolate. Whisk to melt chocolate. When cooled to body temperature whisk in the egg, cayenne and liquor.

Pour batter into prepared pan. Place cake pan into roasting pan. Add water to come half way up sides of cake pan.
Bake until center of cake is set and tester comes out with just a few moist crumbs attached, (about 40 minutes).

Refrigerate cake overnight.

Slip a small fine knife around edge of pan to loosen cake.
Hold pan over hot burner for about 15 seconds to release cake.
Place platter over pan. Hold pan and platter together tightly and invert.
Lift off cake pan, peel off parchment.
Finishing
Place cake on wire cooling rack over a baking sheet.
Use microwave to melt about 1 pound of dark chocolate with 1/4 cup of whatever alcohol you used in the cake. Add about 1/4 cup of cream and whisk chocolate mixture until smooth and shiny.

Pour chocolate mixture over cake allowing it to drip into a smooth covering of top and sides. Gently tilt the entire tray if needed to get even coverage.
Allow to set up in refrigerator for a few minutes. Use long spatula to transfer cake to platter.

BASIC CHEESECAKE

This is a basic cheesecake that is great as is or can be easily adapted with other flavors, adding toppings, where ever your imagination leads you. We used it as the basis for many of the varieties of cheesecakes we made at the shop.

1 Batch
Preheat to 375 degrees
Use paddle attachment

		CRUST
1	Cup	graham cracker crumbs
2 2/3	Tablespoon	sugar
1 1/3	Ounce	butter, melted
		FILLING
1 ½	Pound	cream cheese
6	Ounce	sugar
3	Each	egg
1	Teaspoon	vanilla

Combine the crumbs, sugar and melted butter together for the crust. Press into the bottom and just up the sides of a 9 inch spring-form pan.

Beat the cream cheese and sugar together until smooth and creamy. About 10 minutes on medium if the ingredients were at room temperature. A little longer if the cream cheese was cold. Remember you can beat it as much as you want before adding the eggs.

Whisk the eggs & vanilla then add to cream cheese, mixing only until fully blended.

Pour into prepared crust and bake at 375 degrees for approximately 30 minutes. This is an estimate. The number one reason for cheesecakes to crack is over baking.

 It is done when the middle is still jiggles and wiggles and the edges have risen and rounded slightly.

Remove from oven and allow to cool for 20 minutes before putting into the refrigerator over night to set.

Slide a small thin knife around the side of the pan. Hold pan over a hot burner for about 15 seconds before releasing sides and using a spatula to slide cake from pan to platter or cardboard circle.

Serve as is or top with fresh berries.

THE FRED

This was created early on at the shop and we just called it "that pecan cheesecake thingy". Working next door at the computer shop was a man who started coming in every evening for a slice of the "cheesecake with the nuts". He voiced his frustration one night that he never knew what to ask for when he came in because it had no name. I asked him his name and "The Fred" was born, named for it's first and best fan.

1 Batch
Preheat to 375 degrees
Use paddle attachment

		CRUST
1	Cup	graham cracker crumbs
2	Ounce	sugar
1 2/3	Ounce	butter, melted
		FILLING
1 ½	Pound	cream cheese
6	Ounce	sugar
3	Each	egg
1	Teaspoon	vanilla
		TOPPING
2	Ounce	butter, melted
1 1/3	Ounce	sugar, brown, packed
1 2/3	Cup	pecan pieces

Combine the crumbs, sugar and melted butter together for the crust. Press into the bottom and just up the sides of a 9 inch spring-form pan.

Beat the cream cheese and sugar together until smooth and creamy. About 10 minutes on medium if the ingredients were at room temperature. A little longer if the cream cheese was cold. Remember you can beat it as much as you want before adding the eggs.

Whisk the eggs & vanilla then add to cream cheese, mixing only until fully blended.

Pour into prepared crust and bake at 375 degrees for 20 minutes.

Meanwhile, melt butter for topping, add brown sugar and pecans. Mix well.
Remove cheesecake from oven after 20 minutes. . Carefully spoon pecan topping on top. Return to oven, bake an additional 20 to 30 minutes until done.

Remove from oven and allow to cool for 20 minutes before putting into the refrigerator over night to set.

Slide a small thin knife around the side of the pan. Hold pan over a hot burner for about 15 seconds before releasing sides and using a spatula to slide cake from pan to platter or cardboard circle.

THE LARRY AND PHIL

Larry & Phil were buddies who came in just about every morning for cinnamon rolls and coffee. They happened to work together at MSU as elevator engineers so their job had it's ups and downs. They were cinnamon roll guys and I would give them grief about never getting anything else. They said, "Do something with lots of chocolate and we will." Hence the "Larry & Phil" was born.

1 Batch

CRUST

½	Cup	chocolate cookie crumb
1/4	Cup	sugar
3	Tablespoon	butter, melted

FILLING

1 ½	Pound	cream cheese
3/4	Cup	sugar
3	Each	eggs
1	Teaspoon	vanilla
1/4	Cup	chocolate chips

TOPPING

6	Ounce	semisweet chocolate, melted
2	Ounce	honey,
2	Tablespoon	cream

Combine the crumbs, sugar and melted butter together for the crust. Press into the bottom and just up the sides of a 9 inch spring-form pan.

Beat the cream cheese and sugar together until smooth and creamy. About 10 minutes on medium if the ingredients were at room temperature. A little longer if the cream cheese was cold. Remember you can beat it as much as you want before adding the eggs.

Whisk the eggs & vanilla then add to cream cheese, mixing only until fully blended.

Pour into prepared crust and gentle swirl in 1/4 cup chocolate chips.

Bake until done

Remove from oven and allow to cool for 20 minutes before putting into the refrigerator over night to set.

Slide a small thin knife around the side of the pan. Hold pan over a hot burner for about 15 seconds before releasing sides and using a spatula to slide cake from pan to platter or cardboard circle.

Put the topping ingredients into a bowl and melt in microwave. Whisk until smooth and shiny. Pour the chocolate mixture just on the top of the cake using the round edge of the cake as a boundary. Tip the cake to spread the chocolate evenly. Allow the chocolate to set, then serve!

SECTION EIGHT

Miscellaneous thoughts, trivia and resources or *"I bake therefore I am"* - Good things to know.

The Romans were master bread bakers and baked on top of the stove in either of two ways, **panis artopicius**, *"pan bread"* or baked in an earthenware vessel, as **panis testustis** "pot bread". It should be noted that Roman historians as early as the second century reported that women hated to bake bread and left its baking to commercial bakers. Baking became one of the few means of livelihood allowed to freed slaves. As a freed slave was not allowed to take a job from a Roman citizen only a handful of jobs were permitted to them, baking being one.

Believe it or not the pretzel was the creation of a medieval Italian monk who awarded pretzels to children as an incentive for memorizing prayers. The Latin name for pretzels is *pretiole* and means little gift. The Italian name is *bracciatelli*, meaning small arms, thus pretzels were gifts in the shape of praying arms.

The pretzel is credited with saving Vienna from sacking by the Mongol emperor Babar in the early 16th century. Following several attempts to scale the walls the invaders planned to tunnel secretly under it at night to avoid detection. To ensure freshness of the pretzels the Viennese pretzel bakers worked from midnight to daybreak and so heard suspicious digging sounds and alerted the military. The bakers were awarded their own coat of arms for their part in saving the city. To this day the pretzel is part of the emblem of all Viennese bakers.

Baker's Weather - Stepping out to look at the sky, feel the wind and sniff the air are necessary steps for all good bakers. A change in atmospheric pressure, a downpour, a lightning storm all have an effect on dough, particularly during it's final rising. It is in the final rising that flour is breaking down into sugar and the sugar is breaking down to alcohol and gasses. The weather can have a profound effect on this process and will change the crust, texture and flavor of the bread. As a rule bakers love cool, dry weather as it is easiest to maintain the environment for the dough and yeast under these conditions.

ODD BITS OF BREAD HISTORY

In the middle ages some flours were so coarse (oat and barley in particular) that the baker had to knead the dough with his feet.

Marie Antoinette's actual statement was" Ils n'ont plus de pain, qu'ils mangent de la brioche" "They have no more bread, let them eat brioche"

Tomb paintings from 3000 BC show leavened bread. Another reason why Egypt may have been the first to routinely produce leavened bread is the Nile river. Since earliest times due to silting the Nile has been home to large quantities of Saccharomyces cerevisiae the most commonly used strain of yeast for bread making! Bread baking was such an important social asset that in France it wasn't until the 12th century that King Philip Augustus granted bakers the right to actually own their ovens. Until then they were considered property of the state.

A SHORT GLOSSARY

Ash Content The mineral content of any flour, usually about .5 or .6 percent. The higher the ash content the grayer the crumb.

Batard (literally, bastard) A medium long , oval loaf that is neither baguette nor boule.

Force or Dough strength - this refers to the tendency of dough to pull together during fermentation. While fermenting , dough loses elasticity. A dough that is too elastic will rise poorly and flatly rather than round (usually it was over kneaded). An excessively strong dough holds too firmly resulting in overly round loaves.

Grigne (crusty opening on the surface) Many breads are sliced on the surface before baking. This is to control the break. As the slice expands and browns the opening and raised edge is referred to as the "bloom"

Gluten The element of flour that gives dough its plastic qualities and allows it to hold carbonic gas.

Refreshment Feeding a sour dough starter with fresh flour and water so that it will continue to grow.

Retarder - A refrigerator designed specifically to retard or slow the activity of yeast in a dough.

A FEW BAKING TIPS

If using regular table salt for your baking, cut the amount in half. If possible always use a coarse ground Kosher salt or sea salt. (Salt is used to control the rise as well as add flavor, the fine grind of table salt makes it's effects more intense)

Tapping the bottom or "knocking" of a baking loaf is the surest way to tell if the bread is done, if you get a clear, hollow sound the loaf is ready.

Turning your oven up for the first 15 minutes of baking and then reducing the heat will give your bread an extra "lift" as it rises and help get a crisper crust.

If kneading dough by hand, it is practically impossible to over knead (your arms will give out first). If using a mixer to knead, never set it higher than medium speed and note that very few dough should be kneaded more than ten minutes.

Yeast is alive, it needs moisture, warmth and proteins to grow. It reproduces, creating carbon dioxide which causes bread to rise. Treat your yeast as the living thing that it is and you should have good results. Use fresh yeast (not dry) whenever possible. **All the recipes in this book are based on fresh yeast.**

The quantity of liquid will vary greatly depending on a number of factors effecting flour. Always add your liquid last and treat any amount called for in a recipe as an approximation.

The King Arthur Flour catalog has great resources for the home baker.

Bridge Kitchen supply in New York city is one of the most complete kitchen supply houses I have ever found in this country. Their prices are good and they publish a catalog as well as having a web site.

Great Lakes Gourmet in Novi, MI is a major supplier of pastry tools and ingredients to the industry. Tom and Steve who run it are great guys and have just about anything you can imagine for pastry baking. 1 800 625 4591

The Village Baker by Joe Ortiz is about the best Bread Baking Book out there. (Well, until this one of course)

The Bread Bakers Guild of America has a great web site at BBGA.ORG

You may purchase additional copies of this book by contacting
 Paul Homeniuk at plr567@msn.com or calling 517-337-2297.

Index to Recipes

RECIPE	Page #
Adriatic Potato Soup	62
Ale Bread	13
Alsatian Cheese Soup	63
Babka	14
Baps	15
Barley Bread	16
Basic Cheesecake	91
Black Bread	17
Bogracs Gulyas Soup	64
Borscht Soup	65
Brioche	18
Brotchan Foltchep Soup	66
Cake with Ham & Olives	19
Cassoulet Soup	67
Cheddar with Ham & Jalapeno Soup	68
Chocolate Heart Attack	90
Chocolate Zucchini Bread	20
Chocolate Chip Cookies	89
Ciabatta	21
Cinnamon Rolls	88
Coconut Loaf	22
Corn Bread	23
Cornish Saffron Cake	24
Cream of Tomato Soup	69
Curried Pear Soup	70
Devonshire Splits	25
Ezekiel Bread	26
Farmhouse Loaf	27
Fiesta Chili Soup	71
Forest Mushroom Loaf	28
Gazpacho Soup	72
Herb Bread	29
Honey Whole Wheat	30
Khachapuri	31
Moroccan Bean & Almond Soup	73
Mulligatawny Soup	74
Oatcakes	33
Oatmeal Loaf	34
Pain de Campagne	37
Pain D'Ail	36
Pain au Mais	35
Pan de Pueblo	38

Index to Recipes, continued

RECIPE	**Page #**
Pane alla Cioccolata	39
Panettone	40
Peasant Bread with Figs & Pinenuts	41
Porter Cake	42
Provencale Fougasse	43
Pugliese	44
Pumpkin Bread	45
Roasted Squash, Onion & Garlic Soup	75
Rye	46
Salt Rising Bread	48
Seed and Nut Loaf	49
Sicilian Loaf	32
Simit	50
Soldier's Bread	51
Sopa Al Cuarto De Hora Soup	76
Sour Dough Italian	52
Soyer's Soup	77
Spanish Vegetable Soup	78
Spelt	53
Spicy Red Lentil Soup	79
Spreads	83
Stilton and Walnut Loaf	54
Stolle de Noel	55
The Fred	92
The Larry & Phil	93
Three Grain Bread	57
Tuscan	58
Vichyssoise Soup	80
Vienna	59
Zoldbab Leves Soup	81

MY NOTES ON THE RECIPES I'VE TRIED